CENTRE FOR EDUCATIONAL RESEARCH AND INNOVATION

QUALITY IN TEACHING

ORGANISATION FOR ECONOMIC CO-OPERATION AND DEVELOPMENT

ORGANISATION FOR ECONOMIC CO-OPERATION AND DEVELOPMENT

Pursuant to Article 1 of the Convention signed in Paris on 14th December 1960, and which came into force on 30th September 1961, the Organisation for Economic Co-operation and Development (OECD) shall promote policies designed:

- to achieve the highest sustainable economic growth and employment and a rising standard of living in Member countries, while maintaining financial stability, and thus to contribute to the development of the world economy;
- to contribute to sound economic expansion in Member as well as non-member countries in the process of economic development; and
- to contribute to the expansion of world trade on a multilateral, non-discriminatory basis in accordance with international obligations.

The original Member countries of the OECD are Austria, Belgium, Canada, Denmark, France, Germany, Greece, Iceland, Ireland, Italy, Luxembourg, the Netherlands, Norway, Portugal, Spain, Sweden, Switzerland, Turkey, the United Kingdom and the United States. The following countries became Members subsequently through accession at the dates indicated hereafter: Japan (28th April 1964), Finland (28th January 1969), Australia (7th June 1971), New Zealand (29th May 1973) and Mexico (18th May 1994). The Commission of the European Communities takes part in the work of the OECD (Article 13 of the OECD Convention).

The Centre for Educational Research and Innovation was created in June 1968 by the Council of the Organisation for Economic Co-operation and Development and all Member countries of the OECD are participants.

The main objectives of the Centre are as follows:

- *to promote and support the development of research activities in education and undertake such research activities where appropriate;*
- *to promote and support pilot experiments with a view to introducing and testing innovations in the educational system;*
- *to promote the development of co-operation between Member countries in the field of educational research and innovation.*

The Centre functions within the Organisation for Economic Co-operation and Development in accordance with the decisions of the Council of the Organisation, under the authority of the Secretary-General. It is supervised by a Governing Board composed of one national expert in its field of competence from each of the countries participating in its programme of work.

Publié en français sous le titre :
LA QUALITÉ DE L'ENSEIGNEMENT

© OECD 1994
Applications for permission to reproduce or translate all or part
of this publication should be made to:
Head of Publications Service, OECD
2, rue André-Pascal, 75775 PARIS CEDEX 16, France

Foreword

How to promote good teaching is a central question in all educational systems. It becomes more difficult when conditions are rapidly changing. To gain insight into the dynamic nature of teacher quality in primary and secondary schools, and to exchange information about policies to improve it, eleven countries provided experts to participate in this study under the auspices of the Centre for Educational Research and Innovation (CERI).

In 1992 the researchers met twice to refine the questions and plan the study. These meetings produced agreement on the design of three distinct kinds of inquiry: case studies of policies to improve the quality of teaching, seminars for teachers to discuss the definition of quality and what affects it, and descriptions of new developments in initial teacher education. Teachers and schools were selected for study on the basis of outstanding reputation and evidence of effectiveness in achieving positive outcomes for students. Data collection was conducted in 1993 and the results presented in country reports. In November, 1993 the authors of the country studies, along with other experts, met to discuss the main ideas to appear in the synthesis report.

Chapter 1 of this report places the study in the context of previous OECD work and ongoing reforms of educational systems in OECD countries. Chapter 2 reviews the conceptual framework and procedures used in the country studies, and Chapter 3 describes the samples of schools studied in each country. The case studies, seminars, and teacher education reviews found strong similarities among countries in the attributes and actions of good teachers, presented in Chapter 4. Chapter 5 explains the range of policies to improve teacher quality that were described in the country studies. Implementation of these policies is strongly influenced by the local school context, which also directly affects the quality of teaching itself. Characteristics of schools that support high quality, as revealed by the case studies, are discussed in Chapter 6. Finally, Chapter 7 analyses some of the implications and possible conflicts among initiatives to improve teacher quality that arise from central policies, local schools, and individual teachers themselves.

This report has been prepared by the CERI Secretariat with the advice and contributions of experts. Dr. David Hopkins, of the University of Cambridge Institute of Education (United Kingdom), was the principal consultant on the study from beginning to end, and took primary responsibility for writing Chapters 2, 6, and 7. Professor John Williamson, University of Tasmania (Australia), drafted Chapter 5 and, with Alan Wagner of the OECD Secretariat, Chapter 1. Professor David Stern, University of California at Berkeley

(United States) performed as general editor, and wrote Chapters 3 and 4, while on leave from Berkeley to serve in the CERI Secretariat. Professor Judith Warren Little, also of the University of California at Berkeley, wrote a synthesis of the November 1993 meeting and reviewed the synthesis report in its initial draft.

The report is published under the responsibility of the Secretary-General of the OECD.

Table of Contents

Chapter 1

Teachers and Educational Reform

Origins of this study in previous OECD work	7
New concerns about teacher quality	8
Policies to improve and sustain teacher quality	9
Growing importance of the local context	11

Chapter 2

Conceptual Framework: Quality, Policy and Local Context

The concept of teacher quality	13
Policies to improve or sustain the quality of teachers or teaching	15
Local context of schooling	16
A unified conceptual framework for teacher quality	18
Research approach	20

Chapter 3

Samples and Settings of the Country Studies

Australia	23
Austria	25
Finland	26
France	27
Italy	28
Japan	28
New Zealand	29
Norway	30
Sweden	31
United Kingdom	32
United States	33

Chapter 4

Quality in Teachers and Teaching

Commitment: the driving force	36
Subject-specific didactics: the teacher's craft	41
Love children	42
Set an example of moral conduct	45
Manage groups effectively	47
Incorporate new technology	49
Master multiple models of teaching and learning	50
Adjust and improvise	55
Know the students	57
Exchange ideas with other teachers	58
Reflect!	60
Collaborate with other teachers	62
Advance the profession of teaching	67
Contribute to society at large	69
Conclusion	70

Chapter 5

Polocies Described in the Country Studies

Pre-service teacher education	74
In-service teacher education and staff development	79
Teacher performance appraisal	82
Increased responsibility for individual schools	84
Conclusion	86

Chapter 6

Quality Schools

Characteristics of quality schools	88
Vision and values	90
Organisation of teaching and learning	93
Management arrangements	97
Policy formation process	99
Leadership	103
Staff development	105
Relationships with the community and district	108
Culture of the school	109
Summary and conclusions	112

Chapter 7

Sources of Teacher Quality

Three sources of quality	113
Reconciling teacher, school, and central policy	116
Bibliography	118

Chapter 1

Teachers and Educational Reform

Teachers are at the heart of educational improvement. Any benefits that accrue to students as a result of educational policies require the enabling action of teachers. As the OECD Education Ministers declared at their meeting in Paris in 1990, "Expert, motivated, flexible teaching staff are the most vital component of high quality provision" (OECD, 1992, p. 35). It is for this reason that the OECD, through its Centre for Educational Research and Innovation (CERI), undertook a comparative study of policies aimed at improving teacher quality. Eleven countries participated.

This report presents the main findings of the country studies conducted in 1993. Ten countries contributed case studies on the implementation of policies intended to improve the quality of teaching. Five countries conducted seminars for teachers to discuss the definition of quality and factors that affect it. Five countries provided reviews of particular teacher education programmes.

The particular teachers, schools and institutions described in the country studies were chosen as positive examples of good or innovative practice. This report therefore does not describe the whole range of teacher quality; it focuses on those who are regarded as among the best in each country. Chapter 4 analyses the attributes and activities of these highly accomplished teachers, and chapter 6 examines key characteristics of the schools in which they work. The remainder of this chapter explains how this study was conceived in the context of previous work at the OECD.

Origins of this study in previous OECD work

For some years, teachers – their work, training and conditions of service – have figured prominently in the the OECD's work programme. In the mid-1970s, the Education Committee's Working Party on Teacher Policies addressed questions of the recruitment and training of the teachers required to educate the large numbers of children moving through compulsory schooling. The report of the working party drew attention to emerging issues, some of which resonate today:

> It is by no means evident that existing teacher policies set their short and medium-term measures logically within the context of necessarily more qualitative long-term

perspectives. Nor is it certain that existing mechanisms of personnel planning, programming and management have been able to integrate sufficiently the qualitative and quantitative aspects of development affecting the various categories of teachers and educators (OECD, 1979, p. 12).

The OECD's work identified a key change for teacher policies in the late 1970s into the 1980s:

> The priority given to the effort to recruit enough teachers during the last two decades could now be shifted to allow for more emphasis on quality. The teaching body is now composed of young teachers because of the increased rate of recruitment. These new teachers are due to spend a long time in education. There is little hope of progress without programmes for systematic continuing training. The education of teachers will be at the centre therefore of any programme of educational reform. Fortunately this is a favourable time for changes in the initial and in-service education of teachers (OECD, 1974, p. 9).

Subsequent work in CERI took up this specific challenge, as the focus shifted to issues concerning the organisation, contents, methods and requirements for in-service teacher education (INSET). In reviewing developments in Member countries, the effort gave particular attention to "school-focused" in-service. The final report of the study concluded that the investigation:

> helped to clarify the widely-held view that the traditional INSET strategy, whereby individual teachers attend courses provided by outside agencies, is valuable but too limited and that it should be deliberately extended to encourage teachers and school staffs to plan their own INSET programmes in the light of their self-identified needs (OECD, 1982, p. 29).

In the late 1980s, the Education Committee's Working Party on the Condition of Teaching undertook an assessment of emerging demands on schools and on teachers, developments in the status and motivation of teachers, the evolution of teacher demand and supply, and new tendencies in teacher selection, training and appraisal. The general report of the working party, *The Teacher Today: Tasks, Conditions, Policies* (OECD, 1990) emphasised the need to improve conditions and rewards for teachers, respond to new challenges and demands in education generally, and address the problematic situation in many countries of inadequate teacher supply. The working party identified a new context for teacher policies, one which places the teaching profession "under the spotlight of educational debate and policy" (p. 1).

New concerns about teacher quality

In most OECD countries, concerns about teacher quality reflect new challenges and demands, some of which have appeared as schools and teachers grapple with the consequences of decentralisation. In addition, there are chronic problems of retaining good teachers, and of shortages in specific fields.

The new challenges and demands for schools and teachers emerge from new and heightened expectations of schools, advances in research on teaching and learning and the need to manage classrooms that are increasingly diverse in terms of ethnic, linguistic and cultural backgrounds. These new challenges and demands require new capacities and knowledge on the part of teachers. The current situation is both dynamic and varied. Schools are now being organised in different ways, in terms of both the tasks and the responsibilities assigned to teachers and the differentiation of roles among teachers and between teachers and other school staff. In many countries, teachers' work is now more clearly defined with respect to specified objectives set out for schooling and in relation to the full range of policies and measures taken to achieve these objectives. The breadth of the challenges and demands and the pace of change make the current situation different than in earlier years. Teachers must be able to accommodate continuing changes – dramatic in some countries – in the content of what is to be taught and how it can be taught best. Chapter 4 describes how teachers in eleven countries are meeting these new challenges, and how the definition of quality teaching itself is changing.

At the same time, there are projections in a number of countries of higher levels of teacher recruitment, as the school-age population and staying-on rates increase and larger proportions of the teaching force reach retirement age. But the increased demand for high-quality recruits to teaching has occurred in a situation of problematic status and rewards for teachers in many countries and growing competition from other sectors of the economy. As a result, even in the face of weak employment conditions overall, shortages of teachers persist at specific levels or types of schools, in certain subjects (*e.g.* mathematics, the sciences or vocational/technical) or particular geographic locations.

Policies to improve and sustain teacher quality

The policy and resource implications of all this are considerable. There are doubts about the capacity of programmes of teacher training organised in traditional ways to meet the scale and rate of change of the needs effectively and at an acceptable cost (Wagner, forthcoming). Additional resources will be needed to attract and retain teachers, particularly in areas of persistent shortage, and to upgrade conditions of work and create new career paths.

These considerations have affected the development of new policies and the implementation of reforms in many Member countries. A common feature of recent policy development is that teacher policies have been more explicitly integrated into strategies for the improvement of schooling. Thus, while new policies address long-standing "teacher" issues of pay and class size, they go much further.

In particular, new reforms call for greater involvement of teachers in decision-making and holding teachers accountable for results; provide greater flexibility for teachers to organise teaching and learning in the school (*e.g.* team teaching, use of volunteers and aides, promotion of active learning strategies in the classroom); establish or reinforce different career structures in teaching (*e.g.* advanced-skills teacher, mid-career recruitment into teaching, part-time teaching); and introduce alternatives to and reforms in teacher education (*e.g.* new criteria for selection, school-based pre-service, teacher-initiated or teacher-organised in-service). With the exception of teacher appraisal, where aims and methods are still being clarified, countries already have adopted new directions and specific initiatives in these areas.

In-service teacher education (INSET) has been the primary policy instrument for helping teachers to master their new roles and responsibilities. INSET can be addressed to the entire existing "stock" of teachers, while pre-service programmes can reach only the relatively small flow that enters the profession each year. INSET is therefore a more responsive instrument for accomplishing rapid change. Nevertheless, initial teacher education has important long-run consequences, and countries are using it to bring about lasting reform of educational systems.

Pre-service teacher education is a large activity in its own right. In Europe, for example, it has been estimated that more than 500 000 teachers receive their initial teacher education in over 1 000 separate institutions in which more than 50 000 teacher educators are working (Buchberger, 1992, p. VII). In the United States, it has been estimated that the number of teachers required by public and private schools by the year 2002 will increase from the present 2.9 million to 3.25 million (National Center for Educational Statistics, 1991).

At the most general level it is possible to see a similar three-part content for initial teacher education: subject (content) study, pedagogies including educational theory and methodology, and teaching practice (Askling and Jedeskog, 1993). On the other hand, at the micro level the picture is one of enormous diversity. An examination of teacher education reveals particular national contexts strongly influenced by prevailing political and policy frameworks. For example, in OECD countries (Askling and Jedeskog, 1993; Barbier and Galatanu, 1993) it is possible to see:

- teacher education institutions which are highly autonomous and those which operate within narrow boundaries prescribed by the State;
- the length of initial preparation courses varying significantly: there are some which last more than five years and others that are less than one calendar year;
- teacher education courses (and in-service programmes) located at different levels of the educational system, *i.e.* at the higher education and university level or at the post compulsory level;
- different organisation and structure patterns (*e.g.* concurrent, end-on, integrated, modular) for initial teacher education;
- significant differences in initial teacher education course culture, curriculum and content (*e.g.* a craft model versus a "university" model): the amount of time available for the practice varies from a few weeks to a total of five or six months; students in some programmes need to complete the equivalent of a liberal arts or a science degree before doing education units, whereas in others education studies comprise over 50 per cent of the course;
- that institutions involved in teacher education have very different patterns of organisation (*e.g.* separate cohesive faculties of education compared to those that exhibit fragmented structures), and vary in the size of the student population (from less than 50 to several thousand).

In light of the diversity, one could argue that there are as many teacher education courses as there are institutions offering them. In addition, each course can sometimes have its own rationale which is developed independently from other providers, either pragmatically on the basis of available staff and/or other resources, or on the decision of more powerful members of the institution.

Within each country, the institutions that provide initial teacher education may face conflicting demands. They are usually tied to a higher education system in which rigour and depth of knowledge in subject disciplines is valued above pedagogical skill. At the same time, student teachers are entering a profession in which knowledge of subject matter, while still important, must increasingly be accompanied by mastery of various teaching methods and a capacity to fulfil new roles and responsibilities beyond the classroom. And, like all public agencies nowadays, institutions of teacher education face increasingly stringent budgets and demands for accountability. A description of how some of these institutions are responding to these pressures is included in Chapter 5 of this report.

Growing importance of the local context

A key thread running through the current education policy approaches just described is a new distribution of roles and responsibilities in education, in which the **outcomes** are more explicitly specified and assessed (all in greater consultation with "stakeholders" in the society at large) while the means necessary to achieve them are left more to the responsibility of the individual school, parents and the local community (OECD, 1989).

The approaches have been advanced as part of policies and initiatives variously described as "decentralisation", "devolution", "deconcentration", "systemic reform", "school choice", "school-based management", "local management of schools" and "school development". Whatever the term used or the specific form adopted, the mix of strategies implemented in countries frequently involve one or more of the following features: responsibilities of individual schools have been strengthened; "stakeholders", to include parents, students, communities and enterprises, have taken on some of the responsibilities and roles previously handled by the schools and education authorities; central authorities, in co-operation with parents, students, communities and enterprises, are establishing or reinforcing the means to steer educational provision through the development of curriculum goals or frameworks.

Such changes introduce important, new responsibilities for teachers across a full range of functions – including design of curriculum and instructional methods, allocation of resources, planning and assessment of school programmes. In many places teachers at each school now also exercise more control over their own professional development activities. The nature and implications of these new roles for teachers comprise a central theme in the country studies. Chapter 6 of this report focuses specifically on the local context both as a milieu that defines and influences teacher quality, and as an environment that determines the implementation of central policies aimed at improving teacher quality.

Chapter 2

Conceptual Framework: Quality, Policy, and Local Context

The OECD/CERI study on Teacher Quality was intended to identify the effects of policies aimed at fostering teacher quality, and the conditions under which such policies can be implemented successfully. Building on previous research and practice, the study was intended to broaden the concept of teacher quality as well as to provide guidance for improvements in policy and practice. This chapter briefly describes the conceptual framework that guided the study.

The conceptual framework for the Teacher Quality study consisted of three elements:

- the concept of teacher quality;
- policies aimed at improving or sustaining the quality of teachers or teaching;
- the context of schooling in which policies are to have effect.

Each of these elements is briefly discussed in the sections which follow.

The concept of teacher quality

The changing role of teachers calls for new knowledge and capabilities. Research on teaching and learning appears to give particular emphasis to a deep knowledge of the subject to be taught and an understanding of – and ability to use – a range of pedagogical approaches. Owing to broad social changes (in the cultural and linguistic composition of the school-age population, family structure and female labour force participation rates, among others) and shifts in decision-making in educational systems, teachers are also expected to have a knowledge of the social development of children and of management functions (OECD, 1990). This study therefore began with a definition of teacher quality that encompassed the following five dimensions:

- *knowledge of substantive curriculum areas and content*;
- *pedagogic skill*, including the acquisition and ability to use a repertoire of teaching strategies;
- *reflection* and the ability to be self-critical, the hallmark of teacher professionalism;

- *empathy* and the commitment to the acknowledgement of the dignity of others;
- *managerial competence*, as teachers assume a range of managerial responsibilities within and outside the classroom.

These dimensions of teacher quality should not be seen in terms of narrow behavioural competencies, but more in terms of dispositions. Teacher quality should be regarded as a holistic concept, *i.e.* as a gestalt of qualities rather than as a discreteset of measurable behaviours, to be developed independently from each other. The integration of competencies across these dimensions of teacher quality is thought to mark the outstanding teacher.

These general points are not intended to serve as a fixed, comprehensive definition of teacher quality. Indeed, one of the aims of the study is to elaborate the concept of teacher quality as it is perceived and emerges within the schools being examined in each case study.

Such an "ideal" profile for the individual teacher, however, must be linked both to school, community and country contexts and to the range of abilities, interests, experiences and characteristics now found in the teaching force. Thus, the concept of teacher quality is even more complex than this delineation of dimensions of teacher quality would imply. In this regard, consideration must be given to three aspects of the context in which policies are formulated and implemented.

First, national or local contexts may prize certain objectives or values which alter the balance or mix of the desired dimensions of teacher quality. In different countries, teachers play different roles in the schools and in society, even though all countries share a common interest in ensuring the academic and social development of children. Moreover, it is apparent that national and local contexts are dynamic, reflecting a more rapid evolution of expectations and shifting balances between teacher demand and supply among others. The changes alter the desired mix of the various dimensions of teacher quality over time.

Second, the problematic nature of teacher supply plays a particularly important role. In the face of competition from other sectors of the economy for highly talented individuals, education authorities are finding it difficult to sustain high levels of recruitment from and retention of high-quality teachers drawn from the traditional pool of young college or university graduates. The tightening in the labour market for teachers and the expense involved in developing and sustaining high levels of competence in all of the dimensions of teacher quality have led to a teaching force which is increasingly heterogeneous in terms of the dimensions of quality: some may acquire high levels of competence in all areas, others will be recruited under other criteria (as is the case with mid-career entrants into teaching) and still others will be recruited with lower levels in some dimensions. The implication is that within the teaching pool, teacher quality may reflect varied and differentiated criteria. These different criteria may result from conscious policy decisions to trade off a fixed, uniformly exceptional standard of teacher quality for a teaching force characterised by a range of quality, the latter accompanied by provision of additional resources and support of teaching through other means such as new information technologies or in-service and school development activities (Cross, 1984).

Finally, the circumstances and conditions in the school (to include student backgrounds, parent involvement, available material and physical resources and the "culture" of the school) "define" the scope for effective use of the dimensions of teacher quality just described. In some schools, teachers perform beyond their individual abilities because conditions and circumstances support teaching quality. In other schools, conditions are so unsupportive that high-quality teachers perform below their abilities (Rosenholtz, 1989; Hopkins, 1990).

Schools and Quality: An International Report (OECD, 1989) exposes some of the range of current views of and approaches to the definition of teacher quality. Implicit definitions of teacher quality have been operationalised in standards for selection into teacher training and entry into teaching and in proposed criteria for differentiated career structures and teacher appraisal. These distinctions and differences imply that the concept of teacher quality remains elusive. A major aim of the project was to explore and clarify the array of concepts and practices which define teacher quality.

Policies to improve or sustain the quality of teachers or teaching

National and local authorities have for some time recognised the importance of teacher quality in promoting student achievement. Consequently, many policies have been initiated with this aim in mind. The most common means have been policies related to teacher education, particularly various forms of initial teacher education and the qualifications of prospective teachers. Policies have also extended directly into in-service education, as reflected in CERI's own work (OECD, 1982; Hopkins, 1986; OECD, 1990).

More recently still, the policy emphasis has been broadened from training and development aspects to other means to secure teacher quality. Thus, teacher quality now is seen as the explicit objective of a range of policies, including:
- upgraded, more effective pre-service education;
- upgraded, more effective in-service education;
- teacher appraisal or evaluation;
- alternate paths to teaching posts;
- alternate careers in teaching (including planning and provision for shorter, *e.g.* five years, as well as longer teaching terms; for career progression within teaching; for mobility of employment and benefits into/out of teaching);
- economic and social incentives to enter teaching (including mobility of employment and benefits within teaching; level and differentials in pay and compensation; conditions of work);
- economic and social incentives to remain in teaching (including mobility of employment and benefits within teaching; level and differentials in pay and compensation; conditions of work; strategies intended to encourage resignations or retirements).

The wide range of policy initiatives poses several difficulties. As the concept of teacher quality itself is not well defined, policies tend to have only broad application.

Moreover, policies aimed at teachers may interact with each other and with policies aimed at school quality in ways that dilute the impact on teacher quality. For example, highly talented individuals possibly attracted to teaching through improved career and salary structures may find that more rigid, prescriptive training requirements and certain types of accountability techniques render teaching unattractive. Finally, as already suggested, teacher policy initiatives have their effects at the level of the individual prospective teacher or current teacher. These effects are not directly realised through the policies, but rather work through the broader context as well as in individual schools.

Local context of schooling

The "context of schooling" refers in this study to a range of conditions or factors which are seen as important influences on teacher quality. Teacher policies interact with these conditions or factors, and any examination of the effects of teacher policies will need to take the context of schooling into account. The context includes such elements as:
- *educational policies*, such as curriculum guidelines and strategies aimed at changes in decision-making, which have direct effects on the role and work of teachers;
- *local-level policies and implementation* strategies that affect the levels of responsibility for, support of and direction of the work of teachers in schools;
- *the organisation and culture of the school*, which are seen as independent determinants both of student success and of levels of teacher commitment, co-operation and confidence;
- *the links between classroom and school management,* including collaboration between teachers and the implementation of school-wide innovations, are now seen as crucial to building up teacher capacities as well as improving school effectiveness and student performance. The ability to work in "extra" classroom situations is a new aspect of teacher quality in some places.

Prior CERI work on school improvement gives some indication of the role of the context of schooling on teacher quality (van Velzen *et al.*, 1985, Hopkins, 1987). School improvement has capacity building at the school/local level and student achievement/ teaching quality as its major goals. For the purposes of this project, what is most useful in the school improvement approach is the notion that a range of strategies are identified and used in efforts to realise these goals. The school improvement work suggests that these strategies, individually or in combination, are likely to differ in their effectiveness. The implication is that the effects of teacher policies may differ among schools. Put another way, some school-level strategies may be more effective than others in supporting teacher policies.

Research during the 1970s and early 1980s led to the conclusion that organisational features such as the following tend to characterise effective schools (*e.g.* Purkey and Smith, 1983):

- curriculum-focused school leadership;
- supportive climate within the school;
- emphasis on curriculum and teaching;
- clear goals and high expectations for students;
- a system for monitoring performance and achievement;
- ongoing staff development and in-service;
- parental involvement and support;
- LEA (local education authority) and external support.

However, these factors do not adequately address the dynamics of schools as organisations. There appear to be four additional factors which infuse some meaning and life into the process of improvement within the school. These so-called *process factors* provide the means of achieving the organisational factors; they lubricate the system and "fuel the dynamics of interaction". They have been described by Fullan (1985, p. 400) as follows:

A feel for the process of leadership: this is difficult to characterise because the complexity of factors involved tends to deny rational planning. A useful analogy would be that organisations are to be sailed rather than driven;

A guiding value system: this refers to a consensus on high expectations, explicit goals, clear rules, a genuine caring about individuals, etc.;

Intense interaction and communication: this refers to simultaneous support and pressure at both horizontal and vertical levels within the school;

Collaborative planning and implementation: this needs to occur both within the school and externally, particularly in the local education authority.

As compared with describing the characteristics of effective schools, school improvement approaches to educational change embody the long-term goal of moving towards the "ideal type" of "self-renewing school". When the school is regarded as the "centre" of change, then strategies for change need to take this new perspective into account. This approach is exemplified in the work of the OECD-sponsored International School Improvement Project (ISIP) and the knowledge that emanated from it (van Velzen et al.; Hopkins, 1987, 1990). School improvement was defined in the ISIP as (van Velzen et al., p. 48):

"a systematic, sustained effort aimed at change in learning conditions and other related internal conditions in one or more schools, with the ultimate aim of accomplishing educational goals more effectively."

School improvement as an approach to educational change therefore rests on a number of assumptions:

- *The school as the centre of change.* This means that external reforms need to be sensitive to the situation in individual schools, rather than assuming that all schools are the same. It also implies that school improvement efforts need to adopt a "classroom-exceeding" perspective, without ignoring the classroom.
- *A systematic approach to change.* School improvement is a carefully planned and managed process that takes place over a period of several years.

- *A key focus for change are the "internal conditions" of schools.* These include not only the teaching-learning activities used in the school, but also the schools' procedures, role allocation, and resource use that support the teaching/learning process.
- *Accomplishing educational goals more effectively.* Educational goals reflect the particular mission of a school, and represent what the school itself regards as desirable. This suggests a broader definition of outcome than student scores on achievement tests, even though for some schools these may be pre-eminent. Schools also serve the more general developmental needs of students, the professional development of teachers and the needs of its community.
- *A multi-level perspective.* Although the school is the centre of change it does not act alone. The school is embedded in an educational system that has to work collaboratively or symbolically if the highest degrees of quality are to be achieved. This means that the roles of teachers, heads, governors, parents, support people (advisers, higher education, consultants, etc.), and local authorities should be defined, harnessed and committed to the process of school improvement.
- *Integrative implementation strategies.* This implies a linkage between "top-down" and "bottom-up"; remembering of course that both approaches can apply at a number of different levels in the system. Ideally, "top-down" provides policy aims, an overall strategy, and operational plans; this is complemented by a "bottom-up" response involving diagnosis, priority goal setting, and implementation. The former provides the framework, resources, and a menu of alternatives; the latter, energy and school-based implementation.
- *The drive towards institutionalisation.* Change is only successful when it has become part of the natural behaviour of teachers in the school. Implementation by itself is not enough.

It is this philosophy and approach that underpinned the International School Improvement Project and laid the basis for further thinking and action, including the Teacher Quality project.

The relationships just described can be understood through an example a policy initiative aimed at improving teacher quality. A school may take as one of its own priorities the acquisition of new teaching styles for some its staff. The strategy may be a staff-development programme based on demonstration/practice/feedback, and the conditions that support it are increased staff collaboration. To most teachers, the activity is a seamless coat. If successful, the activity leads directly to increased teacher quality (and improved student learning) and also to changes in the school's organisation (*e.g.* timetabling and the nature of staff development activities) and the school's culture (*e.g.* norms that prize feedback and collaboration).

A unified conceptual framework for teacher quality

The three elements of the conceptual framework are linked, as can be seen by referring to Figure 2.1. The figure is intended to illustrate the linkages and relationships

Figure 2.1. **A conceptual framework for the study of the effects of policies on teacher quality**

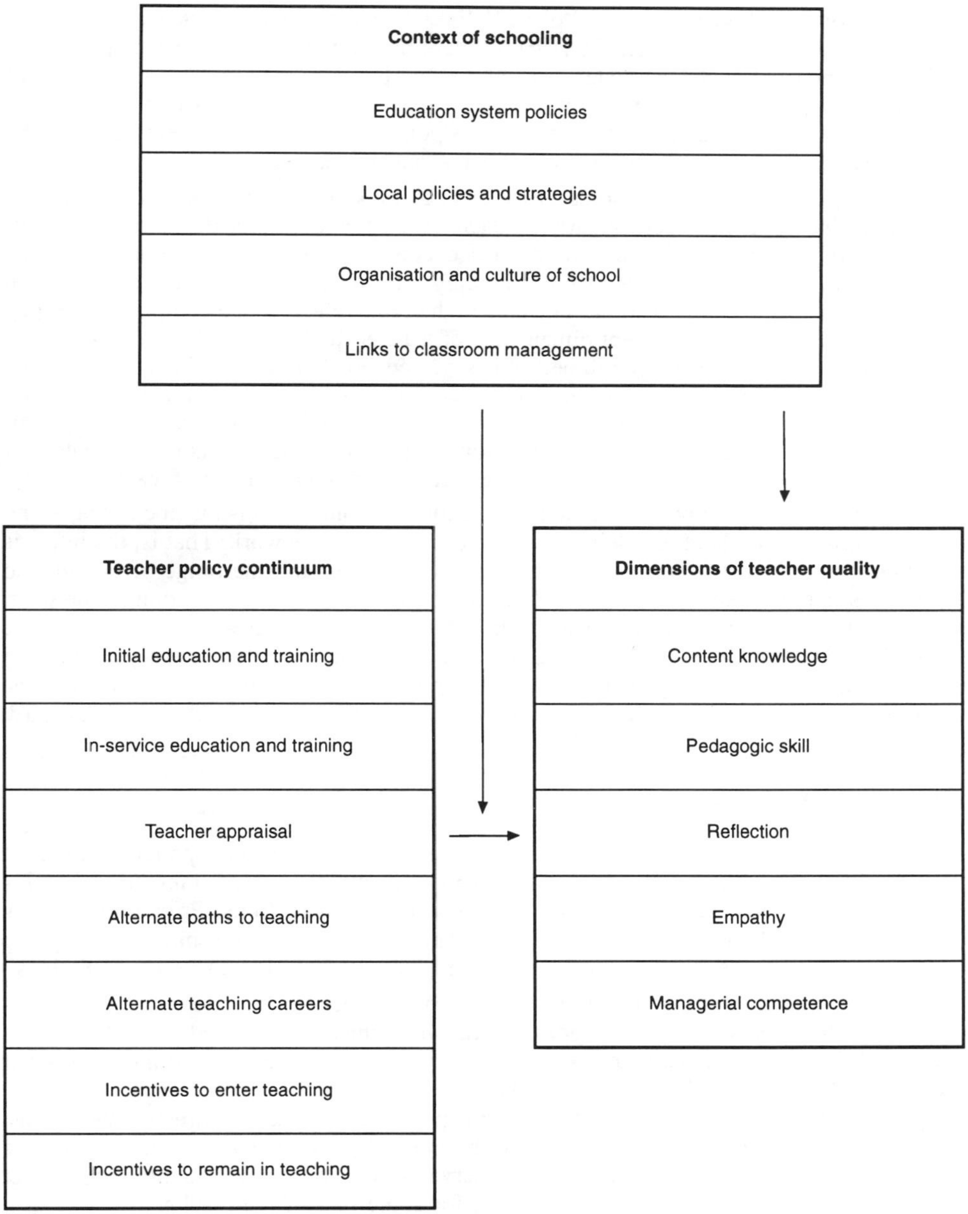

Context of schooling
Education system policies
Local policies and strategies
Organisation and culture of school
Links to classroom management

Teacher policy continuum
Initial education and training
In-service education and training
Teacher appraisal
Alternate paths to teaching
Alternate teaching careers
Incentives to enter teaching
Incentives to remain in teaching

Dimensions of teacher quality
Content knowledge
Pedagogic skill
Reflection
Empathy
Managerial competence

rather than to provide an explicit "model" of interactions and effects. The detailed dimensions, policies and context features shown here are intended to be suggestive rather than definitive.

As shown in Figure 2.1, the "direct" links between teacher policies and teacher quality are implied by the horizontal arrow. Identified dimensions of teacher quality are arrayed on the right, and specific teacher policies are listed on the left. The magnitudes of the "direct" effects of each policy will differ by dimension of teacher quality; for each dimension of quality, different teacher quality policies will have different effects. The contextual factors affect teacher quality directly, and mediate the effects of policies.

The linkages and relationships are more complex, in two respects. First, teacher policies do not operate independently of each other. For example, the effectiveness of particular forms of pre-service and in-service education will differ according to the backgrounds and characteristics of those coming into the profession (*e.g.* via traditional or alternate paths, or as the result of changes in the relative levels and composition of pay and compensation). The different dimensions of teacher quality similarly are interdependent, in that a high level in one dimension (say, pedagogical skill) is likely to facilitate acquisition in another dimension (*e.g.* managerial competence). Second, the effects on teacher quality of teacher policies are likely to be influenced by the "context of schooling", shown in the figure as a set of background dimensions. Elements of the context of schooling can, of course, have independent effects on the improvement of teacher quality.

It should be kept in mind that the figure is intended only to illustrate the linkages and relationships among the three elements of the conceptual framework. That is, the intent is to suggest both how teacher policies affect teacher quality and the range of factors and conditions in the "context of schooling" which need to be taken into account. Moreover, it should be recognised that the discussion here does not specifically consider that the desired levels of and mixes among the dimensions of teacher quality may vary among and within countries and among identified pools of prospective and current teachers. That is, the dimensions of teacher quality do not imply necessarily a single fixed, agreed standard.

Research approach

Because of the complexity in the linkages and relationships, policies aimed at improvements in teacher quality are difficult to research. Traditional methods of policy research do not pick up the range of variables or the interactions. Prior OECD work suggests that qualitative approaches, *i.e.* in-depth case studies or seminar/focus-group activities, are the most appropriate for examining the impact of such policy initiatives.

The approach builds on a line of inquiry which seeks objective, conformable information on the effects of a specific policy initiative. Sometimes referred to as "backward mapping", the technique calls for exploration of the question "What accounts for teacher quality in this school?" rather than "What are the effects of this teacher policy?" "Backward mapping" allows the effects of the policy to be judged indirectly, and against other possible explanations for the results observed. It provides some protection against crediting a specific policy with all of the observed effects on teacher quality, when other policies, conditions or factors might account for some part of the results.

The value of the "backward mapping" technique is illustrated in the following passage, taken from reflections on the Rand "Change Agent" study two decades earlier (McLaughlin, 1990, p. 14):

> Although the Change Agent study correctly stressed the significance of the actions and choices of teachers, and although the study's conclusions underscored the embeddedness of local implementors in a larger system, our conception of the structures most relevant to teachers was too narrow. Our research and analysis took the policy system for granted. That is, we assumed that the structure most relevant to teachers was the policy structure – the federal, state, and local policies – that eventuated in classroom practice. Had we made those assumptions problematic, rather than taken them as givens, we would have seen that although we as policy analysts were chiefly concerned with the policy system, it was not always relevant to many teachers on a day-to-day basis.
>
> This misunderstanding is important because many of the study's conclusions about local responses to change-agent programmes were based on the assumption that teachers responded to specific policy objectives or strategies. In fact, for many teachers these policy goals and activities were simply part of a broader environment that pressed in upon their classrooms. Thus, to ask about the role or consequences of a particular programme or strategy for practice risked misrepresentation of reality because it gave policy a focus or significance it did not have in the daily matter of classroom life. We did not look beyond the policy structure to consider that the embedded structure of greatest import to teachers might have nothing or little to do with policy – it might have to do with professional networks, school departments, or other school-level associations, or colleagues however organised.
>
> Ironically, although the Rand study was among the first to map backward from the perspective of local implementors and to analyse planned-change efforts associated with macro-level policies, it still was a top-down study because the driving questions reflected macro-level concerns, not micro-level realities. Because we did not understand that fully, I believe our analysis fell short as a description of planned change at the local level and as advice to policy makers and practitioners about how to enhance local practice.

The principal analytical activity in the CERI project consists of school-based, teacher-oriented **case studies**. The specific aim of the case studies is to ascertain the ways in which teacher policies, across the range described above, interact in their impact on the dimensions of teacher quality of interest. While the focus is on teachers, the analyses encompassed all staff and the entire school. Schools and teachers were selected on the basis of their reputation for, and in some cases evidence of, a high level of student achievement and a record of continuous improvement.

The rationale for using case studies in the project is the scope they provide for exploring in depth what are quite complex phenomena. Unfortunately, the case-study approach is often associated with methodological problems. Four problems stand out:
– the lack of theoretical frameworks against which to consider issues of teacher quality;
– the variety of sources of data and the way in which they are handled;

- analytical procedures and their link to issues such as validity and reliability;
- the way in which cross-case analysis can lead to the generation of theory and the formation of policy.

In order to help overcome these problems, the project was based on the conceptual framework outlined above which details the dimensions of teacher quality and the impact of policy initiatives and the context of schooling on them. The case studies, while guided by the overall conceptual framework of the project, was characterised by the uniqueness of the individual case. In practical terms, the multi-site case-study design was not limited to a series of case studies of similar policies, implemented in similar ways. Rather, the design allowed for case studies of quite different types of approaches to enhancing teacher quality. As a result, the individual case studies had in common those aspects necessary to enable cross-case comparisons and general analysis, but differed in striking ways according to the characteristics, settings and purposes of the particular approach to teacher quality under study.

Both the conceptual and analytical lines of work already described can be enriched by taking into account teacher opinions and perceptions. This was the purpose of **teacher seminars**. The specific objectives of the seminars were to obtain teacher views on the effectiveness and interactions of policies aimed at improving teacher quality and on the definition of teacher quality itself.

The teacher seminars also permit a type of validation of the findings of the case studies, for those countries in which case studies are prepared. Provision was made in countries participating in both the case-study and teacher-seminar activities to organise one of the seminar meetings around the findings and conclusions of the case study carried out in that country.

The third element of the country studies was a **description of innovative programmes in initial teacher education**. These were intended to indicate the direction of changes in teacher training, to be compared with the conceptions of teacher quality emerging from the case studies.

Chapter 3

Samples and Settings of the Country Studies

After a series of meetings that produced agreement on the conceptual framework and procedures explained in Chapter 2, researchers in eleven countries set out in 1993 to conduct the studies. This chapter describes the particular samples and circumstances that were studied in each country. The actual findings from the country studies are presented in Chapters 4-6. The capsule descriptions in this chapter are meant to convey a picture of the settings in which the evidence was collected.

The studies were of three kinds:
- **Case studies of schools and teachers**. As described in Chapter 2, these were intended to shed further light on the characteristics of high-quality teachers, and the policies and local conditions that contribute to quality teaching.
- **Teacher seminars**. Selected teachers met to discuss definitions and dimensions of teacher quality and how it is affected by policies and local conditions.
- **Teacher education reviews**. These provided descriptions of innovative programmes for initial teacher preparation.

Table 3.1 shows the countries that conducted each type of study. It also shows how many schools were involved and the policies examined in the case studies. Altogether, eleven countries conducted 18 separate studies. The remainder of this chapter describes the samples and procedures in each country.

Australia

Case studies of seven schools were carried out in Australia. The schools were all participatining the National Schools Project (NSP), part of a "co-operative initiative between the Commonwealth Government, teacher unions and State and non-government teacher employers" (McRae, 1993, p. 2). The NSP provided small amounts of seed money to schools, mainly to release some time for teachers to conduct action research on "the links between organisation of work in schools and improved learning outcomes" (p. 3).

Table 3.1. **Summary of country studies**

	Case study		Teacher seminar	Teacher education review
	No. of schools	Type of policy		
Australia	7	Work re-organisation		
Austria	4	Various national	x	x
Finland	5	Teacher and pupil autonomy		x
France			x	x
Italy	4	Student record of achievement		
Japan	1	New teacher induction		
New Zealand	5	School autonomy	x	
Norway	3	School-based curriculum and staff development		
Sweden	6	Teacher in-service	x	x
United Kingdom				
England	4	School-based staff development		
Scotland				x
United States	7	Various local	x	

The schools, all public except one, were:

- Canterbury Public School, serving 330 students in kindergarten through year 6 in Sydney, Australia's largest city. "Canterbury is not a wealthy area. It is close to the major reception centre for immigrants in New South Wales and has a thoroughly cosmopolitan population reflected in the make-up of the school's own population. Unemployment in the area is high" (pp. 10, 14).
- Hincks Avenue Primary School, enrolling 240 students in "reception" (kindergarten) through year 7 in the mining town of Whyalla, South Australia (population about 30 000). A teacher said, "It's five minutes to the bush and five minutes to the sea... but a long, long way from anything else." Unemployment in the town stood at about 30 per cent at the time of the study. "The student population is characterised by a high level of transcience and considerable poverty" (pp. 10, 27-28).
- Phillip College for years 11 and 12, serving 730 students in an inner suburb of Canberra, Australia's capital city. "It draws from year 7-10 schools nearby... These suburbs represent some of the most affluent in Canberra as well as some of the poorest. As a result, Phillip has a student population with a wide range of socio-economic backgrounds" (pp. 10, 42).
- St. Bernadette's Primary School, a Catholic school enrolling 330 students in "preparatory" (kindergarten) through year 6. Located on the fast-growing suburban fringe of Melbourne, the school serves an area with "a number of recently wealthy white and blue collar families" as well as a "substantial pocket of public housing near the school" (pp. 10, 58).
- Sanderson High School, with 800 students in years 8-10, located in a suburb of Darwin on Australia's tropical northern coast. Darwin's population of 80 000 is

"the most racially diverse area of Australia". Students include "Vietnamese, Timorese, Chinese, Indians, Greeks, Maoris, South-Pacific islanders, a significant number of Aborigines, both urban and traditional, as well as many students of multi-racial and multi-ethnic background... Students' families range from wealthy two-income middle-class families to families who have lived for many years with welfare assistance" (pp. 10, 70-71).
- Windsor Gardens High School, for years 8-12, drawing its 620 students from a suburb of Adelaide, South Australia. "About 90 per cent of students are drawn from the immediate district which includes a large area of public housing, now several decades old. The school takes a number of children from surrounding 'shelters' for homeless students, foster homes and institutions. About 15 per cent of the school population is of non-English-speaking background. A range of socio-economic groups are represented in the school, but students come predominantly from the lower end" (pp. 10, 88).

Austria

Case studies were conducted of four schools, from among four of Austria's nine provinces. Regional school inspectors nominated these schools because they were considered at least "clearly above average", or "top quality" (Altrichter *et al.*, 1993, p. 12). The four schools are:
- A primary school in a suburb of Klagenfurt, with 157 pupils spanning seven forms. "The school is considered as highly innovative in that it was in the forefront to implement the new primary curriculum; it also prides itself on its elaborated approach to initial reading and writing, its very active teacher-parent relationships, and its caring child-centred approach" (p. 16).
- A general secondary school (*Hauptschule*, from which most graduates go into apprenticeships, some to an upper secondary vocational school, very few to an upper secondary academic school) in the Tyrol. With only 156 pupils in eight forms, "The school aims for 'joyful learning' of its students and wants to capitalise on its small size" (pp. 16, 49).
- Another general secondary school, this one in the Province of Upper Austria, enrolling 170 pupils in eight forms. "This rural school with a stable staff tries to attract students by developing emphasis in sports" (p. 16).
- An academic secondary school (*Real-Gymnasium*, from which most students continue to the upper cycle of academic secondary education) situated in Graz, the capital of the province of Styria. There are 738 pupils in 29 forms. "The school has a long tradition of high achievement, particularly in science subjects. Recently, the school has also developed a vital school-life and a variety of curricular and extra-curricular offerings which, in part, aim to balance the science emphasis with activities from the humanities, social and political life, ethical responsibility, etc." (p. 16).

In each of these schools, observation and interviews were designed to detect the influence of the following specific national policies:
- including individual teachers and teams of teachers in the preparation, development, and evaluation of regional and national innovation strategies (*e.g.* teams for the preparation of syllabi);
- including teachers (and parents) in the processes of decision-making within individual schools;
- pre-service training of teachers in the fields of education, subject matter methodology, and school practice;
- in-service training of teachers;
- qualification of school principals in the field of school management;
- school-based project work and interdisciplinary teaching within individual schools;
- incentive systems in schools;
- influence of class size on teaching quality;
- specific profiles of schools, commitment to the schools, and quality (pp. 3-4).

Austria also sponsored a **teacher seminar**, which held two three-day sessions. The January 1993 meeting was attended by 18 teachers and six parents, the May meeting by 14 of the same teachers, five of the same parents, and four students who were invited by teachers. Teachers were nominated by provincial school inspectors, parents by national parent organisations. At the first session the participants developed a profile of the "good teacher". After discussion with colleagues and students during the interim, the second session refined the profile and also discussed desirable policies to improve teacher quality (Ribolits, 1993).

Finally, Austria contributed a **description of initial teacher training** at the State College of Teacher Education and the Institute of Educational Sciences, both in Salzburg (Buchberger *et al.*, 1993).

Finland

Case studies of five schools were carried out in Finland. Local and national school authorities selected schools that were "regarded as the best" (Hämäläinen and Jokela, 1993, p. 9). Each school was studied as a whole, with particular attention to one or more teachers at each grade level.
- The Jyväskylä University Training school (327 pupils in grades 1-6) is regarded as a school with a good reputation, because of the fairly high level of the matriculation exam results when compared to the national average. There have been many winners of national and international competitions in the school... Because most of the pupils pass through the lower and upper levels to the upper secondary, the learning outcomes of the upper secondary school pupils can be traced back to the lower level.

- In the Jyränkö Lower Level Comprehensive School (169 pupils in grades 1-4), one teacher's third grade attained excellent results in the reading test of the International Association for the Evaluation of Educational Achievement. The class of the teacher in question was involved in the reading test as a result of random sampling. Because the teacher was still working at this school, it was possible to include her in the study.
- The Moisio Lower Level Comprehensive School in Mikkeli (grades 1-6, 194 pupils) has also achieved a national reputation because of its active development work. The way in which this school has developed itself has been so outstanding and exceptional that teachers and educational authorities from all parts of Finland have visited the school.
- The Halssila Lower Level Comprehensive School in Jyväskylä (418 pupils in grades 1-6) enjoys the high esteem of its pupils' parents as well as that of the educational authorities. The school is regarded as a progressive and continually developing school.
- A small rural school was chosen to represent the 60 per cent of all schools that have one to three teaching posts. The Sointula [not the actual name] Lower Level Comprehensive School (12 pupils in grades 1-6) was chosen on the basis of an earlier survey, which focused on the social participation of teachers in small rural schools (pp. 8-10).

The case studies documented two major shifts in Finnish educational policy. One gives schools and teachers more autonomy, particularly in curriculum development. The second supports a new model of teaching and learning, emphasising "a pupil's ability to seek, process, adapt, evaluate, and understand information" (p. 6).

In addition, a **description of initial teacher preparation** programmes at the University of Jyväskylä was written (Buchberger *et al.*, 1993*a*).

France

France conducted a **teacher seminar** which met for two days in November 1992 and again for two days in May 1993. Thirty teachers participated in the first meeting, of whom 26 returned for the second. Most participants were chosen by regional school inspectors as examples of good teachers. Twelve were teachers at the primary level (*élémentaire or maternelle*), nine were from middle school (*collège*), and nine from secondary (*lycée*). Six had passed highly competitive national examinations to earn the title of *agrégé* in their *disciplines* (Altet, 1993, Appendix 1).

The first session used panel discussions, videos, and scenarios to prompt individual reflection and group discussion and arrive at a working definition of quality in teachers and teaching, with dimensions and indicators. Participants also constructed a survey instrument to collect data from colleagues at their schools before the seminar's second meeting. At the second session the definition of teacher quality was refined and placed in the context of different kinds of schools. There was also discussion of the role of policy and teacher training in improving and supporting teacher quality (pp. 3-6).

France also contributed a study of **initial teacher preparation** in the new two-year university institutes for teacher training (IUFM). Three of these new institutes were described and compared: one enrolling approximately 3 000 students from the region covered by the Aix-Marseille Academy, the second with an enrolment of approximately 3 500 from the Nancy-Metz region, and the third in Picardy with an estimated enrolment of slightly more than 2 000 (Barbier and Galatanu, 1993, Vol. 2).

Italy

In Italy, **case studies** focused on the implementation of a new Record of Achievement for pupils in middle schools. This is a document which teachers are required to complete for each student each year. They must write an assessment and plan for the student at the beginning of the year, appraise the student's performance in all subjects periodically during the year, and record a global assessment again at year's end. The Record is sent to parents and provides a basis for home-school communications. After several years of development and phased implementation, this procedure is now to be required in all Italian middle schools.

Four "good schools" according to inspectors' reports, representing "different geographic and social areas", were included in the study (Macconi, 1993, p. 14):

- Francesco d'Assisi middle school, with 257 pupils, is located on the eastern outskirts of Milan, in a lower-and middle-class residential area. Nearby there is a huge camp for Gypsies, whose presence in the school is not particularly welcomed by parents of the other children. The school has used the Record of Achievement since it was first developed in 1985, because the head teacher at the time was on the national committee for monitoring the experiment.
- Marelli middle school, enrolling 203 pupils, is on the northern edge of Milan, in a lower and middle-class neighbourhood. This school began using the Record of Achievement in 1990, after several years of discussion and study.
- A. Negri middle school enrols 431 pupils in the little town of Vimodromne, near Milan. The working- and middle-class parents "do not consider school the most important feature in the process of education of their children" (p. 23). The Record of Achievement has been in use here since 1985.
- A. Franchi middle school, with 274 pupils, is located on the outskirts of the industrial town of Brescia. The working-class parents "are proud of their school, which helps their children to achieve a higher social status" (p. 24). The school adopted the Record of Achievement in 1990 after evaluation and planning by the teachers. The headmaster is an authority on the Record (pp. 21-25).

Japan

In Japan, a **case study** described a new teacher-induction programme. First instituted in 1988, the programme is now required in all schools. A first-year teacher is given teaching responsibilities, but also receives about two days per week of training from a lead teacher and others within the school, and another day a week at an education centre outside the school.

Implementation of the new programme was studied at Sakura Primary School, which enrols 1 200 students in Sakura City. Many parents and grandparents of the current students graduated from this school, which "plays a leading part in the city" (Maki, 1993, pp. 1-5).

New Zealand

The New Zealand **case studies** described teachers working in a new policy environment. In 1989 New Zealand abolished district education boards and put in their place boards of trustees, each responsible for an individual primary or secondary school. Schools gained increased control over their own finances and management, and in particular over "the purchasing of appropriate resources to sustain quality teaching and learning" (Ramsay, 1993, p. 4).

Nominations for "quality teachers" were solicited from the staff of a regional teacher-education institution. Based on these, and on discussions with others familiar with the schools in the region, five teachers were chosen. All are female, as are more than 75 per cent of primary teachers in New Zealand. Another criterion for selection was that the teachers worked in schools that were implementing "interesting" new procedures "in the area of teacher appraisal and staff development" (pp. 13-14). The five schools and teachers are described as follows:

- Longview is an urban school with 450 students aged 10 to 13, approximately one-third Maori. The school's community reflects all socio-economic groups from professional/managerial to welfare-dependent, though 55 per cent of the pupils have been identified as the lower socio-economic group. The target teacher, with eight years of experience, teaches a composite Form 1 and Form 2 class.
- Ferndown school, in an affluent suburban neighbourhood, has 380 pupils aged 5 to 10, about 20 per cent non-Caucasian, 9 per cent Maori. The target teacher has 13 years of experience, and is currently teaching a composite Standard 3 and 4 class.
- Countryside school, with only 109 pupils aged 5 to 13, is set in a community of farms and small businesses. Many pupils are fifth generation in the school. The target teacher, with 15 years' experience, is currently assigned to a Junior 2 and 3 class.
- Hilltop school enrols 342 pupils in the 5-11 age group from a middle – to low-income suburb. The population is relatively transient. Approximately 20 per cent of the students are Maori. The target teacher, now responsible for new entrants (age 5), has five years of teaching experience.
- Queenwood school, attached to a teacher training institute, enrols 504 students. The school serves a full socio-economic range, with more than 18 per cent Maori. The target teacher, now teaching Junior 2 and 3 (age 6-7), has six years of experience (pp. 14-15).

New Zealand also conducted a **teacher seminar**. Twenty-five teachers were selected by the Practical Studies section of the School of Education, University of Waikato. Two one-day sessions were held, with three weeks in between. The first day dealt with definitions and dimensions of teacher quality, the second with contextual conditions.

Norway

In Norway, **case studies** were designed to document the implementation of new policies contained in the national curriculum guidelines of 1987. These policies provided for local curriculum development, school improvement projects, in-service training, and management development.

Development of local curricula was mandated by the 1987 guidelines, as quoted by Baasland (1993, p. 11):

> The Municipal Education Committee, the individual school and the individual teacher can strongly influence the content of the teaching. The Curriculum guidelines take it for granted that the detailed content and more specific application of subject matter will be decided locally, through the preparation of local curricula and plans of work (...).
>
> The work on local curricula entails developing more detailed syllabi for subjects and topics (...). Each teacher or group of teachers will prepare plans of work for the teaching, based on the local curricula.

The guidelines also direct schools and teachers to carry out school improvement projects. "The demand that the school itself shall initiate and govern development work is part of a model of how experimental and development work in schools should and may be initiated, governed, and implemented. The revised Curriculum guidelines (M-87) introduce a new model for this kind of work. Previously, this was centrally initiated and governed, but was replaced and reorganised so as to be carried out by local participants" (p. 14).

To support teachers' work on curriculum development and school improvement, the national guidelines provide for school-based staff development. The guidelines state that "in-service training [must]be regarded as part of the development work. Further education is partly a prerequisite for development work, and the teachers receive a kind of further training by participating in development work and passing on the results" (p. 17). Baasland notes that "the school as an organisation carries the responsibility for further education...in line with the school's prioritised areas of development work. The school shall survey the teachers' need for further education and improved skills, and also decide priority regarding the use of resources" (p. 19).

Since the 1987 national guidelines "place more demands on planning and coordination at all levels within the schools system", policy has stressed management training and development, for both administrators and teachers. This training also helps teachers within their own classrooms "to involve the pupils more in the decision-making processes and to make them take responsibility for their learning situation" (p. 20).

Implementation of these policies was studied in the municipality of Aurskog-Høland, north-east of Oslo. Three schools were chosen on the basis of statements by local authorities that teacher quality was high and student outcomes had been improving (p. 43). Two primary schools, Aursmoen and Bjørkelangen, enrolled 225 and 193 students respectively. The third school, Aursmoen lower secondary, enrolled 126.

Sweden

The Swedish **case studies** built on a continuing research project begun in 1990. The original aim of the research, which carried into the case studies for the CERI project, was to understand the use of staff development programmes in their school settings. More broadly, the case studies for CERI were designed to analyse teacher quality in the context of local working conditions and the policy environment.

Teachers were sampled from six schools in two districts. One district is located in a rural area near an industrialised city, to which some inhabitants commute for work. Almost all houses are owner-occupied. The second district is in a suburb of a large city. Housing density is high, with a mix of apartments and single-family dwellings (Lander, 1993, pp. 2-3).

Schools were chosen because "their teacher staffs, or parts of their staffs, have been under considerable change for a long time". Two primary and one secondary school were included from each of the two districts. In the suburban district the "schools have rather difficult working conditions, because of learning and social problems among pupils" (p. 1). Schools in the rural district have "relatively small problems" (p. 2).

Interviews or classroom observations, or both, were conducted with 19 primary and 15 secondary teachers (p. 22). The sample excluded teachers who were new to the school, and over-represented teachers who had taken leadership responsibilities among their peers. In the secondary schools, the sample was restricted to teachers of science, social studies, and Swedish (pp. 22-26). Questionnaires were also given to all 84 primary and 61 secondary teachers in these schools (p. 2 and Appendix 5.4).

The Swedish case studies also collected extensive data from students. A "questionnaire was administered to all pupils in grades 5-6 and 8-9 in their own classes during ordinary instruction time. The response rate was 94 per cent at primary level and 96 at secondary level, which means that 350 pupils in grade 5-6 and 400 pupils in grade 8-9 took part". In addition, the researchers conducted four group-interviews with students in grade 9. From each of the two secondary schools, one group was composed of pupils with below-average marks, and the other with above-average marks. Five students were included in each group interview (p. 6).

Sweden sponsored a **teacher seminar** of two days in November 1992 and March 1993. Field staff of the National Agency of Education nominated 24 teachers, evenly divided among those working in large cities and small towns, and among those working a hard or easy social environment (Almius *et al.*, p. 4). The 24 included five primary teachers, of whom two are men; 14 secondary, of whom six are men, and four remedial teachers, all women. Twenty-one came to the first meeting, and 23 to the second (p. 5).

Participants each produced five documents: a professional self-portrait, portrait of a colleague admired for her or his professionality, description of experience in pre-service teacher education, discussion of a recent problem fat work with which help is wanted, and a description of satisfying and dissatisfying conditions at work. The seminar time was spent producing these documents, discussing them in small groups, listening to presentations, and talking as a whole group.

Sweden also contributed a **description of initial teacher preparation**. In 1988 major changes were made in teacher education, "as the last step in the development of the comprehensive school system for all children between 7 and 16 (...). The basic principle underlying the new training programme was the necessity to regard the comprehensive school as a single entity with no streaming of students into different classes and with no marked division of students and teachers into separated stages or levels. All teachers have an overall responsibility for the whole student" (Askling and Jedeskog, 1993, p. 6). Accordingly, teachers are now being prepared to teach a range of subjects, either in grades 1-7 or grades 4-9, with somewhat more specialisation by subject in grades 4-9.

United Kingdom

The United Kingdom contributed a **case study** on the implementation of a new policy for staff development. In England there has been a general devolution to individual schools of responsibility for budgets and programmes. As part of this shift, control over staff development budgets and procedures has also been devolved, within national guidelines. Use of the new procedures was examined in a local education authority (LEA) that had been giving schools significant responsibility for determining their own staff development needs before the new national policy was enacted.

"The area covered by the LEA is largely rural but contains several fairly large towns. As at January 1992, there were (...) 269 primary and 60 secondary schools" (Baker *et al.*, 1993, pp. 9-10). Four schools were identified by LEA authorities as examples of effective practice. All four contain small proportions of pupils receiving free meals, compared to the county average (pp. 32-39):

- School A is a secondary school enrolling 750 11-16 year-olds plus 75 in a sixth-form consortium involving three other schools. The catchment area comprises a small town and a few satellite villages. The local economy relies mainly on agriculture and there is significant unemployment. The school recently became self-governing, which means that parents voted to remove it from the LEA jurisdiction and the school now controls its own entire budget.
- School B enrols 260 7–11 year-olds from a housing estate of privately owned homes on the outskirts of a medium-sized town. Most were said to come from middle-class families.
- School C, with 191 4-11 year-old pupils, is a Church of England school operated by the LEA.

- School D enrols 339 4-11 year-olds, plus 86 in a linked nursery unit. Pupils come from a new housing estate on the outskirts of a small market town, and are said to be predominantly middle-class.

The United Kingdom also contributed a report on **initial teacher preparation** in Scotland (Scottish Education Department, 1992). The teaching profession in Scotland, through the General Teaching Council, exercises more control over initial teacher education than in most other places. The report describes the evolution of teacher education policies and the implementation of current initiatives at the Moray House Institute for Education.

United States

The United States **case study** took place in Fairfax County, adjacent to Washington, DC. The county's population of 843 000 is generally affluent, with the highest median household income in the country; 49 per cent of adults have college degrees. However, the number of foreign immigrants has increased rapidly in recent years, and 30 per cent of the student population in 1992 were members of racial or ethnic minority groups, including 12.5 per cent Asian, 10.2 per cent African American, 7.3 per cent Hispanic (White and Roesch, 1993, pp. 11-12).

The Fairfax County Public School system is the tenth largest school district in the United States, enrolling 138 500 students in 1993-94. The district has enacted several policies to improve the quality of teaching. A teacher performance evaluation programme initiated in 1987 has rewarded outstanding teachers and resulted in the dismissal of "hundreds" for "ineffective performance" (p. 14). Beginning in 1986, the district has promoted school-based instructional planning using results of standardised tests. It has provided curriculum resources and an extensive array of professional development programmes.

Effects of these local policies were observed in seven schools, selected by district staff because they serve diverse populations and appear to be performing well as indicated by a high rate of pupil attendance, rising test scores over the past three years, and an excellent reputation in the community (p. 7). Three primary and four middle schools were studied:
- Meadowlark elementary enrols 547 pupils, with a distribution among racial or ethnic groups very similar to the district as a whole. Approximately 95 per cent of sixth graders pass the Virginia Literacy Tests in reading, writing, and mathematics. Only 8.5 per cent of students receive free or subsidised lunches (p. 36).
- In contrast, Sandpiper elementary, with 443 pupils, has 40.4 per cent qualifying for free or subsidised lunches, and only about 75 per cent of sixth graders pass the Virginia Literacy Tests. The proportion of non-minority students is 52.5 per cent, and 34.6 per cent are African American (p. 41).
- Nightingale elementary, enrolling 623 pupils, is a "special needs school" serving a pluralistic community, with a student body that is 44.4 per cent Hispanic and

31.1 per cent Asian. Free or subsidised lunches go to 70.4 per cent. Nightingale was just made the district's first elementary magnet school, to attract more English-speaking students (p. 46).
- The 1 100 seventh- and eighth-grade students at Eagle middle school are 88.2 per cent non-minority. Only 2.2 per cent receive free or subsidised lunch. The proportions of eighth graders who pass the state literacy tests range from 80 per cent in math to 93 per cent in writing. Students have earned awards for outstanding achievement in the arts and in academic areas (p. 50).
- Heron middle school enrols 750 pupils, 79.2 per cent of whom are non-minority and 11.1 per cent Asian, with 9.1 per cent receiving free or subsidised lunch. A larger proportion of eighth graders, 95 per cent, pass the state test in mathematics than in reading: 89 per cent. The school has an excellent reputation for academic achievement (p. 58).
- Raven middle school is a special-needs school enrolling 762 pupils, of whom 48.3 per cent are non-minority, 26.3 per cent Asian, and 20 per cent Hispanic. Students eligible for free or subsidised lunch comprise 31 per cent. The proportion of eighth graders passing the state test ranges from 55 per cent in reading to 71 per cent in math (p. 64).
- Hawk, another special-needs middle school, contains 981 pupils, consisting of 55.4 per cent non-minority, 26.7 per cent African American, 9 per cent Hispanic and 8.6 per cent Asian, with 24.3 per cent receiving free or subsidised lunch. The proportion passing the eighth-grade literacy test ranges from 65 per cent in reading to 75 per cent in math.

In each school, two to six "teacher experts" were invited to participate in **teacher seminars**. They were "selected because of their active involvement in reflective teaching practices such as teacher research and collaborative decision-making" (p. 7). This group convened for the first time in December 1992 for a one-day meeting to begin brainstorming about characteristics of quality teaching. These were further elaborated in a two-day meeting in January 1993, and the group also discussed the influence of policies (p. 8). At a second two-day meeting in June 1993, teacher experts revised the report of the case studies, wrote about significant points in their career biographies, discussed hypotheses emerging from the case studies about the effects of policies, and wrote about the effect of one policy in their own school. The group met again for one day in October 1993 to review a subsequent draft of the case-study report, and a final meeting was scheduled for January 1994 to hear about the discussion at the November 1993 meeting of country representatives at OECD in Paris (p. 10). These seminars were thus closely involved with the case studies.

Chapter 4

Quality in Teachers and Teaching

It is necessary to attempt a definition of teacher quality so that policies to improve it can be rationally formulated. It is also necessary to recognise that no static, uniform definition of teacher quality is possible. Empirical research relating teachers' behaviour and characteristics to pupils' learning has shed light on certain features of the terrain, but it does not yet illuminate the whole landscape. Perhaps it never can, because the effects of teachers' characteristics and behaviour depend on the background and personalities of both pupil and teacher, and on various contextual conditions, all of which may change over time. In any event, this chapter does not contain any new evidence on the relationship between student outcomes and teacher attributes. Instead, its purpose is to convey the changing and complex nature of teacher quality as documented in the country reports.

Based on existing evidence, the definition of teacher quality presented in Chapter 2 was agreed upon as a starting point for the country studies. To recapitulate, it encompassed the following five dimensions:
- *knowledge of substantive curriculum areas and content*;
- *pedagogic skill*, including the acquisition and ability to use a repertoire of teaching strategies;
- *reflection* and the ability to be self-critical, the hallmark of teacher professionalism;
- *empathy* and commitment to the acknowledgement of the dignity of others (students, parents, and colleagues) in the pursuit of affective as well as cognitive outcomes;
- *managerial competence*, as teachers assume a range of managerial responsibilities within and outside the classroom.

This list of attributes resembles some other attempts to define teacher quality. For example, it corresponds closely to a list constructed by the National Board for Professional Teaching Standards (NBPTS) in the United States, a non-governmental agency created to set standards for certifying expert teachers. The only major dimension on the NBPTS list that was not included in the initial CERI list was that "Teachers are members of learning communities (...) working collaboratively with other professionals on instructional policy, curriculum and staff development'' (NBPTS, 1991, pp. 14-15). This collaborative dimension seems to be increasingly important, as indicated by its salience in the country studies.

The French teacher seminar condensed the CERI list to an elegant threefold definition consisting of "*savoirs, savoir-faire, et savoir-être*" (Altet, 1993, p. 8) – translatable perhaps as "knowledge, knowing how to do, and knowing how to be". The number of dimensions might possibly be reduced still further, to simply knowing and caring.

The main criticism of the initial CERI definition, however, has not been that it contains too few or too many dimensions, but that it is too static. It does not convey the continual flow of interaction through which teachers work. It also does not suggest how teachers' roles may change over the course of their careers. And it says nothing about how the teaching profession as a whole may be evolving.

This chapter attempts to transmit the dynamic character of teacher quality that emerged from the country studies. Vignettes and explanations are presented under a sequence of rubrics that build on the original CERI five categories but also include the dimension of collaboration, along with contributions of teachers to the profession and society at large. The sequence is intended to suggest, very approximately, the way in which individual teachers' competence and responsibilities grow over their professional lifetimes, and also the direction in which the teaching profession as a whole may be developing. This individual and collective development is cumulative and integrative: as teachers acquire new capacities they continue to use the ones they previously had, and as the profession takes on new functions it continues to practise the former ones.

Although it is convenient to group teachers' desired capacities and behaviours into categories, these attributes all interact in practice. As a highly accomplished teacher in New Zealand explained, "other people have rationalised these things into a set of steps and put them into boxes, but really you must work more holistically. Everything to me seems to be out of the boxes" (Ramsay, 1993, p. 55).

Commitment: the driving force

Courage may be the virtue that makes all the other virtues possible, as Winston Churchill reportedly said, but in the case of teachers the quality that makes all other qualities possible appears to be commitment.

Good teachers are engaged in their work. A strong desire to help students learn drives them to keep searching for more effective methods, even when they are confronted by negative attitudes and behaviour on the part of students – a growing challenge according to many of the country reports. Teachers' commitment goes beyond the classroom, drawing them into collaborative efforts with other teachers in their own school and in the wider professional community. Several of the country studies give examples.

The Italian study describes a teacher in action in her middle-school classroom (Macconi, 1993, p. 41):

> She keeps asking, moving along the desks, she wants to have personal opinions, she wants to be convinced, she praises, pushes, involves everybody, goes from a frontal lesson to individualised actions, keeps a steady rhythm, checks time, suggests,

accepts suggestions, sums up and asks questions, she asks for approval or disapproval, requires respect for the person who speaks, she gives clear instructions, in the play she is the key character.

Mainly she gives methods to promote autonomy. At the end of the lesson she sums up and reminds the class about the homework.

The energetic quality of good teaching was also noted in the Finnish study. A primary teacher whose students obtained outstanding results on international reading tests was genuinely interested in her work. "Sometimes I was so excited I completely forgot your [the researcher's] presence." The teacher stated that she has noticed when she behaves enthusiastically the children also become more excited. She added that this enthusiasm is for the most part genuine although occasionally she deliberately acts in this way to motivate her students (Hämäläinen and Jokela, 1993, p. 67).

Ramsay observed, "The common link" among the superlative teachers he witnessed in New Zealand "was their passionate desire for their children to succeed..." (Ramsay, p. 62). One teacher said, "My philosophy is that the basic right of every child is to have the very best that life can offer. Education is the biggest part of it. I am absolutely convinced that if you don't believe in the rights of children and their rights to access learning and knowledge then you are doing them a disservice" (p. 55).

One of the expert teachers who contributed to the United States study wrote about an experience that demonstrates this stubborn, even defiant, commitment (White and Roesch, 1993, pp. 45-47):

I transferred out of sixth grade after 15 years and moved down to second grade in an attempt to "fix" kids before they got to sixth grade in the state that some of them were in (...). The next year I had the opportunity to become part of the Reading Recovery first-grade pilot programme. [Reading Recovery is a model adapted from New Zealand, where classroom teachers are on full-time release to work individually with pupils who are having difficulty.] I jumped at this chance!

The first thing that I learned was that I should not take Keith, a student in my first-grade class, because he only scored at the fifth percentile and probably wouldn't be "successful" in the programme. I was *angry*!... After 16 weeks of lessons, Keith had made *great* strides in reading and writing and was dropping many of his "avoidance" behaviours such as crawling under tables, restroom trips, and frequent and prolonged hand washing. Weren't we making success?

However, Keith was nowhere near "Level 12", the graduation benchmark for this time of year. It was dictated that I should "drop him" and pick another child. But the other four Reading Recovery teachers and I all agreed that all children were being served so *we* decided that I should keep Keith. We simply ignored the paperwork and comments from the Reading Recovery office and proceeded with small but definite steps toward success.

Keith continued to make slow but steady progress. He did not achieve "Level 16" by the end of the year so he did not officially "graduate". So what? He had learned to read and that was a lot more than his older brother, Doyle, had done.

As a classroom teacher, I had Keith again in the second grade. Although I did not meet with him privately each day, I *did* continue to use all of the Reading Recovery strategies with him in the classroom setting.

Keith has continued to flourish. By mid-year, he had shown more than a year's growth as measured by [standardised] testing. Where Keith had always scored significantly below his twin brother on *all* testing, he now scores significantly higher and within grade-level expectations! (The twin brother received only a few weeks of Reading Recovery.) Are these not "significant" indicators? Equally, or even more importantly, Keith *loves* learning, school, his teachers, and his friends. Last week a visitor entered the room and Keith immediately and spontaneously walked up to the stranger and offered to share the story he was writing. He often asks to take a book or his journal home or to lunch. And his "deportment" in class is "above reproach"!

The Reading Recovery office doesn't think that Keith was a success story for Reading Recovery: he didn't "graduate". However, Keith *is* a success. Based on research in developmental learning we *know* that our children do not learn in lock-step based on "clock-time". They take quantum leaps, tip-toe, run in circles, plateau, and sometimes just take a "mental break". The level indicators in Reading Recovery may be appropriate if we look at them over a realistic and appropriate amount of time. Also, every child does not enter a programme equally ready. **We know this**! Why do we dictate that they progress X levels in X weeks? Maybe we should take four weeks to find the optimum learning curve for this child and measure his success and acceleration rate accordingly.

The bottom line is: Keith is a happy, successful, and well adjusted child – **a total child!**

This kind of commitment also came through in written and oral statements by teachers in the seminars that were held to discuss definitions and dimensions of teacher quality. Participants in the Swedish seminar were asked to "write down stories about events or situations in which they had felt great satisfaction about their own work" (Almius *et al.*, 1993, pp. 6-7). Most of the resulting contributions described incidents in which students improved their performance and self-confidence. The New Zealand seminar elicited statements such as, "Excellence in achievement within each child is continually being sought" (New Zealand Ministry of Education, 1993, p. 13); a quality teacher is "self-motivated" and "hungry for challenges" (p. 19), dedicated to helping students become "independent, autonomous learners" (p. 23). Similarly, teachers in the Norwegian seminar spoke about being engaged in the job and taking initiative to develop further competence (Baasland, 1993, p. 41). The French seminar identified "passion, enthusiasm, dynamism" as components of "*savoir-être*" [knowing how to be], one of the three major dimensions of teacher quality (Altet, 1993, p. 8). In a survey of their colleagues conducted by teachers in the French seminar, the category of qualities that attracted the largest number (99 of 144) of affirmative statements was "*la passion, amour du métier, des enfants, l'enthousiasme, développer le désir d'apprendre*" [passion, love for the work, for the children, enthusiasm, to stimulate the desire to learn] (p. 11).

As mentioned, a good teacher's commitment transcends her own classroom. It extends to the school, the profession, and even beyond. The French survey asked about what contributes to schoolwide teacher quality, and found that, after teamwork and common objectives, the most frequent response (77 of 144) was *"une conscience professionnelle ambiante, l'engagement, l'implication, le dévouement"* [a professional atmosphere, commitment, involvement, dedication] (Altet, 1993, p. 14).

An illustration of the power of collective commitment was recorded by teachers in the United States study. As a new approach to integrating special education students (White and Roesch, pp. 72-73), they decided to try forming a team that consisted of one special education teacher and two general education teachers. This team shared responsibility for 75 students, ten of whom had previously been in special classes. One of these, called Fred,

> is a sixth-grade student who had been in [a special] class for the past four years. He is tall, thin, with Coke-bottle glasses and a baby face. He spoke with a high-pitched whine that felt like fingernails on a chalkboard. He quickly informed all of his teachers that his mother has said he couldn't read and, therefore, needed one-on-one [instruction]to complete any assignments. He refused to read **anything** and it was clear that he could not and would not read. He has an extreme penchant for neatness and spent much of his time straightening and organising his clothes and materials. He had no friends, sat by himself in the lunchroom and rarely smiled. He made frequent remarks about being dumb and unable to learn.
>
> Through constant and consistent reassurance, Fred has now achieved specific outcomes including: coming to class prepared with completed homework, improved class participation, independent initiation of tasks, and improved interpersonal skills so that he is not a total isolate. We constantly evaluated ourselves, our strategies and our sanity while continuing to boost Fred's self-confidence. Throughout this period we had biweekly contact with his mother. Fred finally volunteered to read! He also improved his test scores and his grades.

Beyond working together in school, teachers are sometimes called upon to contribute to their communities. For example, in Finland, where 60 per cent of elementary teachers work in small villages where the schools have fewer than four teachers (Hämäläinen and Jokela, p. 76), those teachers must also commit themselves to developing the village community. As one said (Kimonen and Nevalainen, 1993, p. 92), "It seems that I am getting more and more of these municipal and province tasks. At the village level I am in the farmers' association and the village association and I also write for the village newspaper (...). I want this village to rise from here. I am motivated: this is my village. Now that I am here in this village I am serving a greater cause.''

To fulfil their commitments to students, colleagues, the profession, and the community, good teachers tend to work long hours. A New Zealand teacher said (Ramsay, 1993, p. 59):

> I'm fussy about planning and I spend a lot of time thinking things through. Reading about things. Formulating objectives... I am trying to cut down to 50 hours a week. I have operated at 60 hours and it just about killed me. I am no longer coming to school every Sunday; I spend time with my family in the weekends. I'm here at

8:15 a.m., I tend to work my lunch hours because I hate wasting time. I'm here until about 4:30 p.m. on staff meeting nights. My kids at home are in bed by 8 o'clock and I usually work from 8:30 to 11:30 p.m. five nights a week... I am actually working harder now than when I first went into teaching thirteen years ago because I wasn't grown up enough then. Now I want so much more because there is so much more to want. I had an American visitor here recently and she said to me, "You lot are too self-critical. You're never satisfied". I know I am working harder now than in the beginning but I'm getting results so it's all worth it.

An evident hazard for quality teachers is burnout. The Austrian case study succinctly points out (Altrichter *et al.*, 1993, pp. 35-37) that "there are new demands on the schools", *e.g.* :

The increasing dynamics and complexity of social change is asking for "dynamic qualities of students" which would imply some reorientation of the hitherto "static culture of learning in schools". The increasing individualisation in society is "assigning more and more educational and socio-integrative tasks to schools". Yet, at the same time, "many teachers do not feel that they are given better opportunities to fulfil these tasks. They do not feel that the financial endowment of schools has kept pace with the number and quality of tasks assigned to them. Teaching as a profession is perceiving itself to be losing social status, being on the bottom end of the pay scale of comparably qualified professions, and having very few prospects of career and mobility". Some teachers become demoralised. Others, however, find the inner resources to meet the new challenges despite the lack of extrinsic rewards relative to the effort, skill, and commitment required.

A vivid image of teachers struggling with this dilemma comes from the United States report. Teachers from a middle school went away together for an all-day meeting to work on their school plan. A teacher organised the agenda. The meeting started at 7:30. They discussed what had to be done and the problems facing them. Among the problems: students being absent for weeks at a time, with excuses from their parents; small numbers of extremely disruptive students taking too much of everyone's time; too much committee work, contributing to some teachers having to work 12 or 14 hour days for several years; the lack of time during the day for teams to confer; more students who are "aggressive", "independent", "with no supervision", "street wise". The group heard and debated statistics presented by researchers from the district office. They sometimes broke into small groups to work on different components of the plan. "During the day tempers flared and tears were shed briefly as people made suggestions and one teacher snapped, 'Don't make up a committee on this. Don't give me one more damn thing to do!' Breakdowns in the social order resulted in gruff hugs and reassurances. At one particularly intense moment of frustration, a group of teachers announced, "We need singing", and started 'Swing Low, Sweet Chariot'. Everyone joined in, there was beautiful four part harmony and a lingering sweetness and sorrow in the sense of community that had been regained at the end of the song before the discussion started up again" (White and Roesch, 1993, pp. 83-84).

The discussion did start up again. The work goes on. The teachers are committed.

Subject-specific didactics: the teacher's craft

In the classroom, good teachers have to know their stuff and how to teach it. Of the three dimensions of quality teaching identified by the French teacher seminar, one is "savoir" [knowledge] and another is "savoir-faire" [know-how]. Knowing how to convey particular concepts, skills and information to students is what distinguishes good teachers from everyone else. The country case studies provide glimpses of teachers using some of the tricks of their trade.

For example, the Finnish teacher whose pupils have achieved outstanding results on international reading tests carefully chose textbooks that introduce first-grade students to reading and writing simultaneously. She has students write to consolidate their understanding of what they read. She has them write individual story books and a class magazine. These tactics for emphasising understanding and stimulating interest are well known, but this teacher uses them particularly well (Hämäläinen and Jokela, 1993, pp. 68-73).

The Swedish case study offers a number of illustrations that capture part of what Shulman has called "pedagogical content knowledge" (Lander, 1993, p. 64). Briefly:
- A teacher of social studies in a lower secondary school explains that "You can walk backwards into history from today's topics," approaching history from the starting point of current events;
- A science teacher mixes "independent project work, piecework contracting [requiring students to accomplish a certain amount of work but giving them some choice among tasks], and lessons that are more steered by me" (p. 65);
- Swedish language teachers at a lower secondary school have developed a 14-point guide for students writing research papers, *e.g.*, "(5) Consider the order of things to be written about; (6) Do not just read, start your writing as soon as possible; (7) When you have written a paragraph, you can read it to a pal, one of your parents or to a teacher (...). Never borrow from textbooks, summarise with your own words instead; (8) Be careful in noting where all the facts are taken from." (pp. 69-70);
- Primary teachers show pupils how to make "mind-maps", individually or in groups, to organise ideas and information visually into mental categories (pp. 75-77);
- Social studies teachers in lower secondary schools give students routines for starting to construct causal explanations of historical events, *e.g.*, by grouping explanations into economic, social, and ideological (pp. 78-79);
- Swedish language teachers assign students to write descriptions of an event from the viewpoints of different participants (p. 81);
- A teacher of mathematics creates a context for understanding formulas by telling students about the mathematicians who discovered them (p. 82);
- Primary teachers use materials from nature and simple experiments to teach science, *e.g.*, "When we were working with the environmental theme we put garbage in a hole in the soil and observed if it would disappear" (p. 84);

- Primary teachers encourage "free writing" by not correcting spelling and punctuation at first (pp. 87-88);
- Primary teachers use various routines for pupils to talk about mathematical problems, play mathematical games, and apply mathematics to real life (pp. 91-92);
- Pupils in their first year of school need to become sensitive to one another's presence. One exercise for this purpose is to have them sit in a group and count how many there are (p. 98).

Other examples come from the US study. In one incident, a math teacher gives students "Please excuse my dear Aunt Sally" as a mnemonic acronym for the order of arithmetic operations [PEMDAS: parentheses, exponents, multiplication and division, addition and subtraction] (White and Roesch, 1993, p. 75). An English teacher engages students in discussion of whether there really are only three different basic plots in all literature (p. 77).

Again, some of these tactics are well known and widely used. Some are simple devices, while others are sophisticated sequences requiring deep understanding of how students learn. In fact, good teachers are able to use their specific subjects as opportunities for pupils to learn general skills such as critical thinking or expository writing. "Subject-specific didactics" therefore overlap with the general models of teaching and learning described in a later section of this chapter. Here the main point is that these tactics are the teacher's special stock in trade, and a high-quality teacher will have a large repertory of effective gambits at his disposal.

However, building an extensive repertory is not easy, especially when teachers are constrained to follow a prescribed curriculum leading to a uniform examination. For instance, in the French seminar teachers in upper secondary schools (*lycées*) were concerned about their own lack of pedagogical training, and did not know how they could make their material more interesting to students while at the same time preparing them to take the national *baccalauréat* examination.

Love children

Feelings of affection between teacher and pupils help create a positive attitude toward learning. Good teachers try to communicate warmth, even if pupils do not reciprocate. The country studies noted numerous instances. For example, the Italian study described three middle school teachers (Macconi, pp. 40, 42):

Warm voice and high tone, she easily smiles, greets warmly entering the class, she actively interacts, she keeps close to pupils and constantly walks in the classroom, tells then to keep their backs straight, she praises, rewards, ... follows her pupils even after they have left the middle school.

With difficult children, she gets close, helps them using verbal and non-verbal codes. She often praises and considers a mistake a resource from which to learn.

Quiet and gentle tone of voice, a bit of humour and irony, he does not leave anybody out, carries along all students. He is on the stage but he is not the main character. A feeling of pleasantness and well-being in the class. Pupils look at him as an adult companion. They go to him privately.

In a middle school in the United States, similarly positive relations were observed (White and Roesch, 1993, p. 80):

As I walk through the hall between classes I see teachers standing in the hall in front of their rooms. Students greet them as they pass: there are high fives [handshakes], eye contact and big smiles...

Through the week I have been alert for discipline and management problems, racial or ethnic tensions among the students. I am impressed by what I don't find. I see no overt hostility between adults and students in this school. The teachers don't complain about or bad mouth students, which surprises me after years of service in other schools in which an us-them mentality reigned in the teachers room and war stories of "horror" students abounded. A physical education teacher that I observe spontaneously announces, for example, that, "These are good kids. They are the best. There is no fuss. They know what to do", as she organises them to work on their physical fitness exercises. I see many small acts of affection as, for example, a teacher reassuring a frightened looking student on the day that report cards go home; another teases a girl about her detailed knowledge of the soap operas. Students in an English class solicitously ask a teacher if her cold is any better... and somewhat teasingly reassure her that they will be good that day even if it is Friday because she looks like she doesn't feel very well. When teachers discipline in class, the language used by the teachers is crisp, matter-of-fact, not personally demeaning, and over quickly: "I have two gentlemen who are making an incorrect choice. I'll let them correct it before I have to" (p. 81).

In contrast to schools at other times and places in which frustrated teachers have had adversarial relationships with students who were seen as uncontrollable, hostile, or unable to learn, these teachers talked about and treated even their most troubling and troublesome students with empathy, respect, and dignity (p. 84).

A Swedish primary school teacher told how she struggled to overcome her own antipathy toward some children. "My idea is that you can't achieve anything if you don't like every pupil and, at the same time, this may be hard. Then you have to work hard with yourself. It's mostly a boy who's the trouble, and if I reject him, then it will go bad. No, I have to fight against myself. You must not feel a little child as an enemy or a threat. He is a little kid and I am the grown-up" (Lander, 1993, p. 36). Similarly, teachers in Swedish lower secondary schools faced with "authority-testing" by students, tried to deal with students as individuals, gave them plenty of praise, and treated them as adults-to-be (p. 43).

Quality teachers observed in New Zealand showed extreme patience and perseverance, supported pupils' self-esteem, and used humour (Ramsay, 1993, pp. 56-60). One teacher said, "You've got to have a sense of humour (...). You must understand children's sense of humour, too, and work with them on it. Having a good laugh is a tonic for everyone" (p. 58). Teachers modified the physical environment of their classrooms to make them cheerful and comfortable, and they emphasised children's desire to feel safe and secure. "If the children are to take risks with their learning, there needs to be a secure base. They need to feel safe before they'll take a chance. If they think I'm going to punish them for getting it wrong they'll become cautious learners", explained one teacher. Another agreed, "For some kids you might be the only adult to smile at them. And if the children know you care they'll take risks" (p. 62).

The teacher seminars in several countries affirmed the importance of positive affect. In France participants listed "bienveillance, écoute, empathie" among the components of "savoir-être" (Altet, p. 8), and especially for pre-primary and primary teachers noted the "Importance primordiale des relations humaines, de la relation psycho-affective avec les élèves" (p. 15). The Austrian seminar wrote, "Teachers respect the individuality of pupils and parents and take their wishes and need seriously; teachers guide pupils in developing self-confidence" (Ribolits, 1993, p. 11).

Risk-taking by students was an explicit theme again in the New Zealand seminar (New Zealand Ministry of Education, 1993, pp. 19-20):

> One concept which was often repeated was that of risk-taking. Children should firstly experience an environment in which there are opportunities for risks to be taken, but also one in which there is sufficient security such that risk-taking does not result in adverse consequences.

> Good teachers build self-confidence, self-esteem, and feelings of self-worth in students by creating opportunities for them to succeed. There are few places as judgmental as a classroom. Students are constantly under scrutiny, are continually being assessed, and are regularly having their progress compared with some norm or with those two covert qualities – ability and capacity. Concern is expressed if students fall short, a concern which students often internalise as negative feelings about themselves and their competence. Good teachers regulate learning tasks and challenges on an individual basis so that every student can and does succeed. The bridges between acquired knowledge and desired knowledge are always manageable. And it is the knowledge that they can achieve which gives students the confidence to attempt and succeed in the next learning challenge.

What taxes teachers' compassion is the fact that needy children are not all passive and dependent. They may be actively disruptive. The Swedish seminar report gave ten examples of difficult students (Almius *et al.*, 1993, p. 16). Here are four of them:

> I have a child in grade 7 who can't sit still for two minutes. He talks unceasingly. He disturbs the whole group and also me. He influences others to behave in the same way in spite of the group's attempts to calm him down.

> A girl in the class has weird relations to the others. She starts rumours about others, she conspires and affects the spirit negatively in many ways. She is afraid herself, yet she has power over others.

> A mentally strong boy in grade 7 has established himself as leader of a gang of four "weak" boys. He makes them neglect school work, but he does the homework himself.

A boy has been in constant conflict with his peers during his time in school. He has no real mates, but terrorises younger children. He lies and cheats his way out of every situation. He has had foster parents for some time since his mother is dead and his father an alcoholic. The father still carries on a lawsuit to protect his rights over the boy, and he does not want to co-operate with the school. The school leaders do not involve themselves actively except in very acute situations.

To sustain teachers' capacity for benevolence in the classroom, some schools have instituted practices to help students feel liked and respected. The Swedish case study describes outings and shared social projects which the children do not see as schoolwork and which indicate to them that adults really want to be with them. For example, one teacher relates, "We often walk out in the woods, having adventures together. We make fruit soup and grill sausages in improvised ways, just for the feeling of effort together" (Lander, 1993, p. 39). Inviting students to participate in parent-teacher conferences has a similar intent (pp. 50-51). In an Australian high school where the curriculum is divided into many units to give students a great deal of individual choice, "pastoral care groups" have been formed to give students an emotional home, which the atomised curriculum might not otherwise provide (McRae, 1993, pp. 80-82). Teachers' love may be strong, but it is not indestructible, and measures like these can give it some protection.

Set an example of moral conduct

Good teachers are concerned not only with pupils' intellectual growth, but also with the development of moral character. In some countries, this is also an explicit objective of public schooling. For example, the compulsory schooling law in Norway states (Baasland, 1993, pp. 6-7):

The purpose of primary and lower secondary education shall be, in agreement and co-operation with the home, to help to give pupils a Christian and moral upbringing, to develop their mental and physical abilities, and to give them good general knowledge so that they may become useful and independent human beings at home and in the society. The school shall promote intellectual freedom and tolerance, strive to create good forms of co-operation between teachers and pupils and between school and home.

In France, the survey conducted by participants in the teacher seminar revealed a clear sense among teachers of an increasing responsibility for pupils' social and personal development, due to declining strength of the family (Altet, 1993, p. 20).

Teachers help strengthen students' moral and personal character not by lecturing about principles, but by setting an example. This was one of the characteristics of high-quality teachers identified by the Swedish teacher seminar: "respect the children and act as a distinct model for them" (Almius *et al.*, p. 19). For instance, the Swedish case study described how teachers intervene in conflicts among the children, setting limits, showing alternatives, and acting as "the leader of the flock", as one teacher put it (Lander, 1993, pp. 36-37). Similarly, the Finnish primary teacher whose pupils achieved outstanding results on international reading tests (Hämäläinen and Jokela, 1993, p. 68) told researchers that:

pupils should learn to respect one another in spite of the differences between them. The teacher directs the pupils' attention to this principle and together they explore ways in which this principle can be realised. One such method involves not laughing at one another's mistakes. The teacher has explained to the pupils that everyone makes mistakes and there is therefore no reason to laugh. She also endeavours to act as a model. If she shows that she respects all pupils equally it becomes easier for the children to do the same.

Sometimes a whole school can support children's development, when teachers are consistent in their principles and behaviour. For example, a middle school in the US case study (White and Roesch, 1993, pp. 65-66) is described as:

> a joyful, warm, and caring school. At all of the meetings, teachers and administrators seemed least anxious, most calm and reflective in the face of what were often serious problems and sometimes personal tragedies. (While I was there they held a ceremony to celebrate the life of a student who had died earlier in the year in an automobile accident.) There was much emphasis on both student accountability and choice. Yet as compassionate and caring adults, the teachers seemed steady and wise, able to laugh both at themselves and at the foolishness and mistakes of youth, acting up now but who, it was assumed, with proper guidance would emerge from this trying developmental period as stronger, solid citizens.

The Austrian teacher seminar (Ribolits, 1993, p. 9) added a dimension they called "social awareness" to the five-fold CERI list of major dimensions in quality teaching. Among the specific aspects of this dimension are the following:

> Teachers are aware of the social function of the school, *e.g.* the distribution of life opportunities ("lower/higher education").

> Teachers are aware of their own gender-specific socialisation and know that their behaviour is a product of socialisation; they critically analyse this role behaviour in various forms of further education.

> Teachers create democratic structures which grant a genuine say to pupils with regard to contents, classroom design, approaches, etc., and thereby foster the classroom community.

> Teachers are aware that scientific findings are never disinterested but depend on the political and ideological beliefs of the scientist.

The New Zealand case study also brings up the issue of social equity. "Issues of race, class, and gender were reflected in everyday life in classrooms. As [two of the teachers] put it, sexism and racism had to be acknowledged by students and detrimental consequences understood and dealt with... In one classroom a teacher inadvertently put together an all-girl group. A student was overheard to remark, 'That's not very gender-sensitive, is it?' The situation was quickly remedied" (Ramsay, 1993, p. 61).

In this last incident the teacher not only adhered to a principle of gender sensitivity. She also demonstrated willingness to respond to a point of principle put by someone with less power.

Manage groups effectively

In the standard classroom, a teacher works with 20 to 40 students at a time. The interplay of individual personalities creates an unpredictable sequence of events. Animating and channelling this flow of interactions comprises much of the teacher's art.

The Austrian seminar thus declared that high-quality teachers "know how to handle group-dynamic processes..." (Ribolits, 1993, p. 12). For example, in a whole-group, frontal teaching format, teachers have to respond when students interrupt with irrelevant talk. The Swedish report describes teachers in this situation "making it a skill to joke pupils back to the official aim of the lesson" (Lander, 1993, p. 41).

Each group develops a distinct personality, as a Swedish teacher observed:

"Classes have a spirit of their own, a kind of mentality of the class as a group. In some you feel the good co-operation and their good working-habits. In others you feel their nervousness and tension. You can feel this within a few minutes." Another teacher added, "It's something magical. Sometimes, and in certain classes, you get a feeling which is light, nice, relaxed. Sometimes it's impossible" (p. 44).

A class with a negative personality can make a teacher's life very difficult, as one of the Swedish secondary school teachers described:

I now have a class that has had a hard time at upper primary. Life in the classroom has been so disturbing, so interrupted by tensions that pupils never could develop a sensitivity for each other or for instruction that puts some demands on their patience. They act very egocentric, they only listen if they hear their own names mentioned. When they don't understand, they immediately interrupt and take all attention, they can't bear to follow my reasoning half a minute more, even if I tell them to wait and see. Many of them are so stressed, and they disturb everyone else.

The first semester with them I had to deal with these problems almost every lesson, talking about their time at the upper primary. We had crisis meetings. The pupil-care staff intervened for individual pupils, and the working-unit discussed their problems. I presented my ideas and got support from my colleagues. I have been a kind of lawyer for these pupils I now have learned to know as individuals. My colleagues believed in me, and now have a better understanding of the pupils (p. 44).

In addition to whole-group instruction, teachers also have students work individually and in small groups. As compared to whole-group instruction, teachers perceive these other formats as allowing pupils to learn at their own pace (Lander, 1993, p. 90). A simple example is individual silent reading, as described in a particularly well-functioning US sixth-grade classroom (White and Roesch, 1993 p. 66):

The start of the school day seems so effortlessly efficient and easy. Both the teachers and students use well known routines so that there are no reminders or repetitions of announcements... [The teacher] says, "Let's drop what we're doing and start to read." Every student has an article or a book out on their desk in which they immediately become absorbed. I am amazed: no fights or whining, "I don't have a book". The room is silent for twenty minutes with just the sounds of twenty-some calm relaxed student bodies and their teacher breathing and turning pages.

Individualised instruction also takes more complicated forms. In Sweden, primary teachers and teachers of Swedish at the secondary level were observed to make widespread use of "piecework contracting" based on a document called a "planning schema". For certain periods of time, pupils are free to choose among a set of agreed-upon tasks. Their efforts become "more task-regulated than clock-regulated" (Lander, 1993, p. 103). At the end of one or more weeks, pupils hand in their schemas with a report of what they have accomplished. Some teachers have students report orally, in small groups. Teachers write comments on the completed schemas, which may also be taken home to parents (pp. 57-61). These individualised contracting procedures in the early grades prepare students for larger independent projects later.

Instructional formats other than frontal teaching add a logistical dimension to the group-management problem. For example, a Catholic primary school in Australia decided to involve students in setting their own individual goals. The problem then was scheduling a goal-setting conference for each student. To free up students' and teachers' time, teachers increased their use of silent reading, project work, language groups, trips to the library, and prayer time (McRae, 1993, pp. 67-68).

An implicit or explicit purpose of individualised and small-group instruction is to let students take greater responsibility for their own learning. This devolution of responsibility from the teacher to the pupils is viewed with approval in the reports from several countries. The Austrian seminar recommended that teachers relinquish some of their leadership and "encourage pupils to develop their own managerial competence" (Ribolits, 1993, p. 12). Similarly, in the New Zealand seminar, "Purposeful cooperative management between teacher and pupils was seen to create a collective ownership and thus less teacher domination" (New Zealand Ministry of Education, 1993, p. 33). The physical arrangement of tables and chairs in the classroom supports and symbolises the sharing of responsibility. Lander (1993, pp. 35-36) notes that:

> None of the observed classrooms in primary schools had the teacher's desk placed in classical front position before the pupils' benches. It was usually placed in the corner not far from the blackboard and often occupied by working materials. The placement of the teacher's own table underlines symbolically that her management functions do not need a "royal" status in the focus of everybody's attention and from where she herself with an eagle's eye can supervise everybody at the same time. In fact, all teachers observed were constantly walking around or sitting close to pupils except for the rather few moments when they did blackboard work.

The Italian case study also observed that the classrooms of high-quality teachers "are organised in a non-traditional way so as to establish more empathy and a non-authoritarian relationship even at a non-verbal level" (Macconi, 1993, p. 39).

Some teachers involve students in deciding what subjects to study and what methods to use. A primary teacher recounts (Lander, 1993, p. 63):

> We often plan social and natural studies for one or two weeks. We decide on a topic, which pupils often can influence – shall we take North America this time, or shall we continue with the human body? I think ahead and discuss with them about their interests, so that I can adjust my suggestions. Sometimes they want me to lecture, sometimes they want to work in groups. They are very fond of doing individual booklets, *e.g.* about Africa. They sometimes write up to 50 pages.

Secondary teachers in the Swedish study also give students questionnaires to obtain their opinions about the effectiveness of various instructional exercises and formats (p. 66). In addition, Swedish students are also given responsibilities not related to instruction, *e.g.* serving lunch and cleaning up afterward (p. 40).

Working with younger pupils is another responsibility given to students in many Swedish schools (p. 38). In classrooms that combine pupils whose ages vary by more than one year, cross-age tutoring is an "organisational corner-stone" (p. 99).

However, there is no mention of cross-age tutoring in the description of the small school in rural Finland, where nine pupils in grades 3-6 are taught in one group, with another group for three pupils in grades 1-2. Here the two teachers can personally attend to the individual needs of each pupil, though the co-ordination of individual and group instruction is still complicated (Kimonen and Nevalainen, 1993, p. 86).

Incorporate new technology

Computers in classrooms are no longer a novelty. Good teachers now are expected to incorporate the use of computers and other digitised-information technologies into their repertories. As more powerful hardware supports more creative educational software, the opportunities for using computers expand. The case studies provide some examples of teachers upgrading their use of technology.

A teacher at one of the middle schools in the US study was a member of a team sent by the school district to Harvard University for a one-week training workshop on using technology to support student inquiry. Back at her school, the English teacher taught a more powerful word-processing programme, the math instructor demonstrated the use of visual organisers for large data sets, and students were enabled to use bibliographic data bases (White and Roesch, 1993, pp. 53-54).

At a US elementary school, a lesson is observed in which "the teacher uses a laser-disk programme to show students selected prints by Matisse. The students discuss the 'shapes' and the patterns that they see. Math is integrated as they relate known math concepts such as symmetry, shapes, parallel and perpendicular lines to the prints. Students do cooperative art as they create Matisse-like art work with water-colors, crayons, cut shapes, and a computer graphics programme. A follow-up lesson included writing poetry based on the patterns" (White and Roesch, 1993, p. 42). Here the use of technology is artfully interwoven with other methods.

Teachers in an Australian high school decided to use information technology as the basis for an integrated curriculum designed to help year 8 students, who were having difficulty making the transition from primary school. The students involved succeeded in learning keyboard skills and how to use all the available computer programmes. In addition, the use of computers "soared" among students and staff generally. "The computer suite (with no game programmes) is used heavily in class time, at lunch-times and after school" (McRae, 1993, p. 100).

At a Finnish school that enrolled 194 pupils in grades 1-6 (Hämäläinen and Jokela, 1993, pp. 57-58), there were "21 computers in daily teaching use (...). Computers are used in almost every subject and project":

> An interesting use of computers is the system of electronic mail which is widely used in the school. With the help of electronic mail, contacts can be made both nationally (*e.g.* with other schools) and internationally (*e.g.* "Tele-Olympics"). At the moment pupils are working on a project called "Spring is Coming" through the electronic mail. Schools situated in different parts of Finland are in this project and they send each other messages about how the spring is approaching in their area. The extent of Finland from north to south offers an excellent opportunity for such observation because spring arrives in different parts of Finland at very different times. The pupils go out to observe trees, lakes, fields, plants, animals and people and then the collected data is sent through the electronic mail system to other schools. In [this] school there is a large wall atlas on which all the areas involved in the project are marked. The most recent information on the approach of spring in different areas is taped by the map so that all the pupils of the school can observe the information.

A sixth-grade teacher at this school is currently carrying out research on the use of computers in teaching (p. 48).

As noted by teachers in the French seminar, use of technology can help motivate pupils (Altet, 1993, p. 24). In some settings, teachers must keep incorporating new technology in order to keep up with their students!

Master multiple models of teaching and learning

The professional teacher not only has at her command an array of tactics for teaching particular concepts, skills, and information. She also has developed a theoretical and practical understanding of different pedagogical models or philosophies. In the country studies two such models were evident in addition to the standard model of whole-class instruction with the teacher at the centre of attention. One alternative approach treats the individual pupil as a a semi-autonomous learner, working at his own pace, to some extent asking his own questions and choosing his own tasks, under the guidance and supervision of a teacher. The other alternative model organises learning as a social activity, in which small groups of pupils collaborate.

The country studies provide numerous examples of teachers treating pupils as semi-autonomous learners. This philosophy is particularly well established in New Zealand, which (Ramsay, 1993, p. 26):

> has a distinctive pedagogic style in primary schools built up over many generations of teachers. The approach has carried various labels at various times, but fundamentally it is child centred with an emphasis on grouping of children for a range and variety of activities, coupled with an individualised approach with a considerable amount of non-directive teaching leading toward independent learners who own their knowledge. This is not to say that New Zealand teachers avoid full class

directive teaching – the expository style is used but in conjunction with a range of other teaching and learning styles tailored according to the teachers' judgements of individual children.

Ramsay traces the development of this philosophy from the 1920s to the present. In 1961, for example, the view which already prevailed was encapsulated in guidelines from the Department of Education, which advocated classroom "work in which the child is discovering for himself, with the aid of the teacher and his classmates, the solutions to problems and difficulties encountered in the pursuit of purposes which he accepts as his own".

Contemporary echoes of this philosophy can be heard in a number of statements in the report of the New Zealand teacher seminar (New Zealand Ministry of Education, 1993, pp. 12-13). For example:

Quality teachers are facilitators. They deliberately engineer situations with learning in mind. They orchestrate classroom environment, and environments beyond the classroom, to effect desirable change, that is learning, in students. Quality teachers (...) are instruments allowing students to achieve their goals through them.

A teacher in the Swedish seminar made the point that students must learn to think for themselves because all knowledge is provisional and approximate. "It is important to convey clearly to pupils what knowledge is – a model for formalising and describing reality. That the collecting of knowledge is a transitory process, a house of cards built up just to be demolished and then rebuilt again. We ought to spend more time teaching the children to ask questions about reality, instead of presenting the expected answers" (Almius et al., 1993, p. 21).

A high school in Australia has constructed its entire curriculum on the principle of self-directed learning. Instead of the standard sequence of courses ordered by year level, it offers dozens of "units" and gives every student wide leeway in choosing six to study in each ten-week term. According to the school's Staff Handbook, this "vertical timetable", as it is called, "treats students as individuals, allows for variety in students' progress, gives the opportunity for students to advance quickly and to pick up subjects missed or unsuccessfully completed earlier, as well as enlarging the number of courses offered without reducing the quality or academic value of any subject" (quoted in McRae, 1993, p. 77).

In France the traditionally dominant approach has been more subject-centred and less student-centred than in some other countries. However, French teachers apparently see this changing. The survey by participants in the teacher seminar found a consensus that the new teacher is more "*centré sur l'élève, sur ses méthodes d'apprentissage, un animateur qui donne le goût d'apprendre, (...) s'adapte, se met au service de l'élève, diversifie ses pratiques, un guide, médiateur dans l'acquisition du savoir, capable de fournir une aide méthodologique, quelqu'un qui apprend à apprendre et forme l'esprit*" [centred on the pupil, on his learning methods, is a stimulating person who cultivates the taste for learning, (...) adapts himself, puts himself at the service of the pupil, varies his methods, is a guide, a mediator in the acquiring of knowledge, able to provide methodological help, someone who teaches how to learn and forms the mind] (Altet, 1993, p. 20).

The dominant philosophy of teaching is also reported to have changed in Finland during the 1980s. "At the beginning of the 80s the dominant view was that the [curricular] goals defined the teaching. At the end of the decade the pupil became the centre and the deciding factor." In the new view, the teacher "creates situations favourable for learning, directs them, and questions them with a constantly fresh perception". Recommended practices include "discussion-based teaching, independent work, pupils' own projects, and social methods (...). Punishments and rewards are rejected, and learning-by-heart is not favoured. The metacognitive skills of the learner are practised" (Buchberger et al., 1990a, p. 10).

The Finnish case study gives several examples of this philosophy in practice. At one school for pupils in grades 1-6, "pupils are given the freedom to plan their own work independently, to carry it out individually, and also to evaluate their own work for themselves (...). Up to half of the lessons are based on pupil-selected tasks, during which the pupils work individually. To achieve this, every pupil makes a regular weekly plan for himself". Teachers give pupils initial ideas with which to work. There are also some tasks that are compulsory for everyone, but pupils still have a choice about how to accomplish them. They can work when and where they wish, but tasks must be completed in time for a "sharing lesson", which usually takes place on Friday (Hämäläinen and Jokela, 1993, pp. 50-51). This school's practice was inspired in part by the French educator Célestin Freinet, but it is not a true Freinet school. A parent said, "in this school, study is for life" (p. 58).

In contrast, the teacher at another Finnish primary school whose pupils did exceptionally well in international reading tests follows a much more conventional curriculum, using ready-made textbooks and workbooks. However, she also emphasises the development of pupils' ability to work independently, even in first grade. "The intention is for pupils to take responsibility for their school work and to work without a need for constant supervision. This aim was successfully achieved in the class which was investigated although the pupils had been in school for less than a year. The pupils did given tasks very independently and they tackled extra assignments without prompting from the teacher. When the pupils entered the classroom after break they immediately began to undertake tasks of their own accord" (p. 66).

The three other Finnish schools described in the case study also practised individualised, student-centred pedagogy in various ways. At one, there was an emphasis on active experimentation by pupils and integration of different subject disciplines (pp. 24-28). At another, teachers in second grade were experimenting with contract-based learning (pp. 43-44). And at the small rural school, individualisation was almost inevitable because there were only 12 pupils for two full-time teachers – although parents in the rural community were sceptical about project-based learning and wanted "a traditional school, the school they have had in their time", according to one of the teachers (Kimonen and Nevalainen, 1993, p. 87). Thus all five of the Finnish schools chosen as examples are practising a kind of pedagogy centred on the individual pupil, despite considerable differences in other respects.

The definition of "pedagogic skill" proposed by the Austrian teacher seminar is also thoroughly student-centred. "Teachers allow pupils to assume responsibility for their own learning process (...) encourage pupils to perform a self-evaluation of their talents and weaknesses (...) respond to pupils' individual needs (arousing and retaining curiosity; promoting independent and action-oriented work) (...) promote learning and work by discovery, by research, through processes and the senses (...) grant sufficient time and create flexible free scope (...) promote pupils' self-reliance (...) provide for opportunities of relating theoretically acquired knowledge to lifetime situations'' (Ribolits, pp. 10-11).

The Austrian national authorities have issued decrees favouring project work in secondary schools and pupil-centred learning in primary schools (Altrichter *et al.*, pp. 20-21, 1993). In one of the case-study schools, an academic high school with a strong reputation for achievement in science, the introduction of project-based learning by the previous head ''aroused a lot of conflicts'' because some teachers saw this as undermining traditional methods (p. 29). But the current head has managed to reconcile the two philosophies.

Motivating pupils tends to become more difficult in secondary school, where the curriculum in most countries divides pupils' time into discrete periods for study of the separate disciplines. The Swedish case study rated pupils' commitment as observed in classroom behaviour. ''Focused work by most pupils most of the time'' or ''almost all pupils deeply committed all the time'' were seen in 86 per cent (18 of 21) of the primary classroom observations, but in only 39 per cent (11 of 28) of the secondary classroom observations. Instead, the majority of observations in secondary classrooms witnessed ''most pupils committed to work some time, but unevenly and with little enthusiasm'', or else ''passivity, only occasional work'' (Lander, 1993, p. 53).

Although Swedish secondary students do experience some pupil-centred instruction, evidence from the Swedish case study (Lander, p. 5) suggests that they would like more of it. Group interviews with ninth-grade students in two Swedish secondary schools probed their perceptions of good teaching. Both high and low achievers:

> define good instruction (by which you learn important things) as incorporating a certain kind of pupil's working pattern. This involves independent (sometimes including co-operative) searching for and formulating knowledge, aiming at producing some tangible result. They often call it ''making own work'' or ''doing research''. Pupils also include good lecturing with instructive explanations (...). They also talk about the need for variation and their interest in dramatising the research product or simpler parts of the skill acquisition.

Regression analysis of questionnaire responses from pupils in grades 5-6 and 8-9 also revealed that ''interesting instruction'' was the strongest predictor of a positive attitude toward school. ''Interesting instruction'' was a scale composed of answers to five questions indicating how often pupils find school work exciting and interesting, like what they are doing in the classroom, feel learning is fun, and enjoy the interesting things they are learning about. The measure of positive attitude toward school was based on four questions indicating whether pupils really want to go to school every day, like to be at school, feel happy there, and get along well at school. Interesting instruction was a better predictor than any other variable, including measures of the pupil's social integration at school, academic self-esteem, and several aspects of teacher behaviour. Pupils who most like going to school are those who are most excited by what they learn there (Lander, 1993, pp. 12-16).

This probably explains in part why teachers observed in the Swedish case study have been developing individual learning contracts, planning schema, and project-based learning (Lander, *e.g.* pp. 55, 61). These methods stimulate pupils' interest because they can choose their own topics and methods, work at their own pace, and make what they learn personally meaningful.

As distinct from the model of instruction centred on the individual learner, another model views learning as a social activity. Group learning can enhance students' motivation by embedding learning in a social context. As Lander points out, "Meaningful contexts are almost always social" (p. 41). Some forms of group learning have been found effective in augmenting pupil achievement in OECD countries (Slavin, 1993).

This approach also appears in several of the country studies. In Norway it was endorsed by the 1974 national curriculum guidelines, which emphasised that "teachers should apply more variation in methods of work" including "group teaching (...) Co-operation activities are stressed – to co-operate and learn to co-operate is in itself an objective" (Baasland, 1993, p. 5).

Some individual teachers have adopted co-operative learning on their own, without any institutional support. One of the middle-school teachers in the Italian study exhibited a flexible repertory of strategies for grouping students, and also "has developed a system of tutoring among peers" (Macconi, 1993, p. 40).

The expert teachers observed in New Zealand made frequent use of co-operative learning (Ramsay, 1993, pp. 46-47). For example, in one classroom:

> The children have been issued calculators and they are to work in pairs. [The teacher] gives the following instructions: "The 4 and 6 buttons on your calculator are broken. I want to know how you can make up 24. Remember you are not allowed to use the 4 and 6 button. Try it out." The children begin working furiously on their calculators and discussing in their pairs how they can come to an answer. As they reach a possible solution, they put up their hands. "All right, we'll start with you," says [the teacher]. [A whole-class dialogue with the teacher ensues, and several alternative solutions are given.]

> [A short time later, the teacher] moves to a fresh problem. On a prepared card which she put on the whiteboard she had this written out: "After weighing all the children in Room 9, Mrs. Smith said she thinks that the girls are generally heavier than the boys. Is this true or false and how can we find out for sure?" [She] then supplies the children with a list of their names and their weights. She asks again, "How can you prove it?" One boy responds by saying, "Sort out the boys and girls, put all the boys on one side of the paper and the girls on another, and begin adding."

> "Yes, that's perhaps one way of doing it," said [the teacher]. "Move to a buddy and come up with a way that shows I'm telling a lot of 'hog-wash' or if what I've said is true." The children then proceed in pairs to try and solve the problem. Peer teaching and co-operation in pairs is emphasized.

Cooperative learning is also increasingly common in the United States, perhaps especially among younger teachers. A first-year teacher in one schools was congratulated by his principal for having given "one of the best co-operative learning lessons I have ever seen" (White and Roesch, p. 61). Mathematics teachers recognise the importance of having students talk about their reasoning. For example, in one math class students went to the blackboard to show solutions to homework problems that other students had asked to see. The teacher later told the researcher, "I love to hear the students explain the problems to each other. That is so important!" (p. 76).

Another teacher (White and Roesch, 1993, pp. 52-53) wrote about how a group-learning structure helped a student with a learning disability become more confident as a writer:

> One of our strategies in the teamed class was cooperative learning. During the Chesapeake Bay Animal/Food Web project, Bobbie was chosen by his group to be the writer. He took his job very seriously. He asked for help because he wanted to do a good job. When he finished writing, he asked the teacher to check his spelling. He had asked the teacher to type his report on the computer, but actually was able to type it himself. We could see he accepted his role as a writer and was very proud of his accomplishments. Since that time, Bobbie is much less reluctant to write.

In this example, role-playing provided motivation for a student to improve in one of the basic academic skill areas. Lander (1993, p. 107) notes that role-playing also can improve metacognitive skills.

Adjust and improvise

Models and philosophies have to be implemented in a changing environment. Good teachers are quick to improvise on the spur of the moment. They also accept and embrace long-term change.

Participants in the French teacher seminar admired teachers with "ouverture, créativité, humour et équilibre personnel" (Altet, 1993, p. 8). Their survey of colleagues found the second most often cited characteristic of a quality teacher was "*la capacité d'adaptation aux élèves, au système, au monde extérieur, aux supérieurs, la remise en cause permanente*" [the ability to adapt to the pupils, to the system, to the world outside, to superiors, the constant calling into question]; and the third was "*l'ouverture d'esprit*" [an open mind] (p. 11). Similarly, one of the Italian expert teachers remarked, "Today you are expected to be able to negotiate and change in different contexts. It is not always easy" (Macconi, 1993, p. 34). And the New Zealand teacher seminar declared (New Zealand Ministry of Education, 1993, p. 27):

> Good teachers have the confidence to do the things they believe in; they are prepared to change − not change for the sake of change − but they actively seek change based on their philosophical beliefs. They have the ability to reflect on what is being done and to accept necessary changes if it is believed they will be of benefit. Such teachers are never passive with change: they seek it and confront it and at times create it.

An anecdote written by a US teacher (White and Roesch, 1993, p. 31) illustrates another teacher's ability to improvise in the face of a sudden surprise:

The class was comprised of six students whose ages ranged from 8 to 13 years. This was a class of students who had been identified as Emotionally Disturbed, were prone to violent outbursts, and who hadn't had much in the way of success, academic or otherwise, in school.

The teacher had all the students seated at a horseshoe table around a blackboard and began the lesson by handing each a card containing a sentence with no punctuation. Just as she asked, "What's missing from your sentences?", a gentleman knocked on the door, [explained that he was there to saw a hole in the door to make a window], and began to saw [with a power saw]. The teacher laughed. The students who appeared to take their cues from her also laughed. She proceeded with the lesson by using sign language, dancing around with the sentences, writing instructions on the board and asking the kids to reply on the blackboard.

Those kids didn't take their eyes off the teacher. Meanwhile the saw continued to buzz and sawdust was flying everywhere. By the time things quieted down, the lesson was just about over. The teacher finished the lesson in much the same fashion as she began. When the students were informally quizzed about what they'd learned about quotation marks and the punctuation within quotes, it was discovered they'd really learned something!

A similar example in the US study was a math class where the power went out, leaving the room dark. "Not knowing how long the power would be off, the teacher calmly begins to call out math problems for the students to do in their heads to review for an upcoming test" (p. 60).

The quality of improvisation with humour was illustrated in this example from a New Zealand lesson on poetry (Ramsay, 1993, pp. 51-52):

Teacher: "I'm going to use a favourite of mine..."

Alex: "Will you read this one to us first?"

He hands her a book.

T: "I don't like this. I won't read it. I know why you want it read."

A: "If you won't, can I?"

The children laugh. They obviously know what's in store.

T: "All right then, you can read it. Here's the book."

A reads: "Glory, glory, alleluja,
Teacher hit me with a ruler,
I hit her on the chin
With a rotten mandarin,
And her teeth came marching out."

Everyone shares the joke, including the teacher. It's all accepted in good humour. The lesson bubbles on with the teacher reading a poem about teeth, and challenges the children to write about another part of their body. She asks for suggestions.

John: "My gurgling stomach."

Donna: "My lovely knees."

The ideas flow, with much laughter as the lesson proceeds.

The Finnish teacher whose class scored high on international reading tests, and who followed a well-structured plan based on conventional textbooks, nevertheless emphasised the importance of being "flexible when necessary. She explained that the daily life of the school is full of various events (...) which alter the original plan (...). The teacher stated that the pupils are also more important than any teacher's plan. For example, if the teacher noticed an argument between pupils, this would be immediately resolved even if it took up lesson time" (Hämäläinen and Jokela, 1993, p. 64). New Zealand teachers' knack for responding to events while maintaining a focus and strategy was admired by Ramsay, who remarked that their "ability to intelligently observe their pupils in action and plot the next move for them placed them at the level of a grandmaster in chess" (p. 54).

In addition to nimbly navigating the ongoing stream of events, teachers must also master long-run trends. In particular, students are changing in many places. Smaller proportions come from stable, two-parent families, among other trends. The US case study describes a teacher's momentary surprise when students were assigned to do research about their own ethnic groups and one boy said he did not know his ethnic group because he was adopted. The teacher's suggestion: talk about the ethnic background of his adopted family (White and Roesch, 1993, p. 62). In another school, teachers grapple with an apparent increase in the number of students whose parents have lost control of them (pp. 82-83). In a similar vein, an Austrian teacher complained that teacher training institutions are not preparing new teachers to contend with students' "behavioural problems" (Altrichter *et al.*, 1993, p. 18). These teachers, and others like them, are coming to grips with social forces originating outside their own sphere of control.

Know the students

Increasingly, teachers must come to know their students as individuals. One reason is that the diversity of the student population is increasing in many places. One middle school in the US case study, for example, enrolled children from 37 countries who spoke more than 20 languages (White and Roesch, 1993, p. 64). Second, teachers are making more use of instructional models centred on individual pupils, as described above. Third, as Lander points out (p. 101), the "social distance" between teachers and pupils has diminished, in conjunction with a broad societal trend.

Italy has undertaken the most systematic policy to ensure that teachers know their students as individuals. The Record of Achievement for each middle school student is an individual planning document. Teachers must write a global assessment of each pupil at the beginning of the year, with recommendations for that pupil's programme of instruction. Performance in each subject is recorded at intervals during the year, and another global assessment is written at year end (Macconi, 1993, pp. 15-16).

The recent reform of middle schools in France also has enabled teachers to take greater account of pupils' individual differences, to diversify their instructional practices so that a maximum number of pupils can remain confident and successful (Altet, 1993,

p. 17). "Savoirs psychologiques et sociologiques sur l'élève" are listed among the attributes of quality teachers at any level (p. 9).

In one of the primary schools described by the Finnish case study (Hämäläinen and Jokela, 1993, p. 29), teachers:

> continuously share information about pupils during the time they are at the school (...). This means that when the pupils' teacher is changed (...) the new teacher and the pupils have already met during earlier years. This process of getting acquainted occurs in practice in that the teacher of the upper grade already teaches his future pupils during earlier grades. This may be on an occasional basis or he may also teach a certain subject regularly. Teachers also try to maintain a certain knowledge of pupils through discussions with one another.

Personal relations between pupils and teachers tend to be closer at primary than at secondary level, where responsibilities and relationships are more fragmented. This was explicitly discussed in the French and Swedish teacher seminars. In Swedish secondary schools one teacher is designated as "superintendent" for each class to help create more personal ties, but Swedish seminar participants regretted that the potential benefits of this arrangement are often not fully realised (Almius *et al.*, 1993, p. 31). One aim of the 1988 reform of initial teacher education in Sweden was to prepare new teachers to share "overall responsibility for the whole pupil" (Askling and Jedskog, 1993, p. 9).

To know the pupil, it helps to know the parents. In Norway, where the 1974 national curriculum guidelines called for instruction that takes "the pupil's individual abilities as its point of departure", the 1987 revision underlines, among other things, the necessity for co-operation between school and home (Baasland, 1993, pp. 5-6). Improving communication with parents was one of the expressed purposes for introducing the Record of Achievement in Italian middle schools, and there is evidence that the purpose has been achieved (Macconi, 1993, p. 29). One of the Finnish schools studied is especially open to parents, and has even used parents' responses on questionnaires in planning its instructional programme (Hämäläinen and Jokela, 1993, pp. 37, 40-41). The exemplary teachers depicted in the New Zealand study also cultivated close ties with parents, welcoming their telephone calls at home and their presence in the classroom and on field trips (Ramsay, 1993, p. 59). The New Zealand seminar report drove the point home (New Zealand Ministry of Education, 1993, p. 13):

> Good teachers do not separate the classroom from the home and the parents, they see the relationship as one of partnership and endeavour to work with parents in the best interests of the child. Students spend about 1 000 hours per annum at school out of a total of 8 760. Those 7 760 hours when another environment is at work must be and are taken into account by the quality teacher.

Exchange ideas with other teachers

It is not possible to become a good teacher without talking to colleagues. Some of the exchange is through formal presentations; most occurs through informal conversation. Both are important for teachers' professional development.

The United States case study found formal interchanges in the form of "teachers preparing and giving school, area, state and national workshops and in-service courses, as well as teaching occasional courses at a nearby university and writing for publication" (White and Roesch, 1993, p. 85). The academic secondary school in the Austrian study is a national centre for in-service training of information technology teachers. Of the 85 teachers at the school, "about 20-30 of them are part-time teacher educators at the regional teacher training colleges, 10-12 do part-time lecturing at one of the regional universities, and many have taken part in regional or national working groups, *e.g.* for the preparation of the new information technology syllabus" (Altrichter *et al.*, 1993, pp. 16-17).

Formal procedures for exchange among teachers within a school were observed in some studies. Three schools in New Zealand had teachers working in pairs to interview each other, then observe in each other's classrooms and discuss what they saw (Ramsay, 1993, p. 21). Teachers at two schools in Norway were reported to have practised "colleague counselling" (Baasland, 1993, p. 42). At the primary school in the Austrian study, a first-year teacher was collaborating with an experienced teacher, who gave her teaching materials and helped with preparation (Altrichter *et al.*, 1993, p. 25). In Japan (Maki, 1993, pp. 6–7) a formal teacher-induction programme gave new teachers 60 periods of instruction by more experienced teachers and administrators in their own schools, covering the following contents:

Current topics in education: educational aims and objectives of the school; school climate... (7 periods).

Instruction: participation in practical study on teaching and learning process; observation of model teaching, practice of teaching plan; preparation for teaching subjects and curriculum construction (24).

Student guidance: profound understanding of individual students by means of educational counselling, case studies, comprehension of strong and weak points of each student, coping with the misbehaviour of students (6).

Classroom management: coping with the various problems confronted by the classroom teacher; effective plan of classroom measurement; significance of home visits by the teachers, etc. (5).

Practical skill: effective management of school business related to teaching, keeping to the Public Service Regulation; dealing with the time book and attendance record, weekly teaching plans, classroom accounting, practice of emergency treatment, management of school pool, etc. (10).

Other training: contents of moral education, special activities, coping with external organisations like PTAs (8).

Informal exchanges among teachers are not directly observed in the case studies, but teachers talked and wrote about how important they were. Most of the vignettes written by teachers in the Swedish seminar describing their own successful experiences explicitly acknowledged the help of one or more colleagues (Almius *et al.,* 1993, p. 10). A social studies teacher in one of the high schools included in the case study remarked, "In this department we talk much about ideas and how we design content-areas. That's the best inspiration we have in this job! We don't work together so closely that we do things together, but we talk a lot" (Lander, 1993, p. 139). US teachers also testified to the importance of colleagues for their professional development (White and Roesch, 1993, p. 22):

> Much of my growth was the result of other people taking the time to observe what I was doing, encouraging me to do more and telling me when what I was doing was worthwhile.
>
> My team (...) has helped me expand my knowledge into interdisciplinary curriculum ideas and strategies.
>
> All the way along, there were people who supported me, taught me, pushed me, invited me.
>
> Undoubtedly, the association with my colleagues, the areas of expertise that each brought to the workplace and the sharing that happened so naturally, has kept me constantly learning myself.
>
> The final major influence on my professional development is the power of the team I work with. They energize you and force you to be the best that you can be.

The French seminar included knowing how to communicate with colleagues among the attributes of a quality teacher (Altet, 1993, p. 10), and the primary teachers in particular spoke of the importance of learning from one another's experience (p. 15). The New Zealand seminar likewise noted that teachers' "reflection is assisted by discussion and verbalisation with colleagues as the search for sense and understanding goes on" (New Zealand Ministry of Education, 1993, p. 16), and also that peer observation can be a useful practice (p. 28).

The principal of the university training school described in the Finnish study has encouraged teachers to discuss educational issues, providing books and magazines for that purpose (Hämäläinen and Jokela, 1993, p. 23). This can be seen as an attempt to elevate and institutionalise the informal dialogue that appears to be so valuable for teachers, creating a "critical community" for checking one another's observations and ideas (Altrichter et al., 1993, p. 9).

Reflect!

Since Donald Schön published *The Reflective Practitioner* in 1983, there has been widespread agreement that teachers should engage in reflection. Of course good teachers have always thought about what they do, but Schön's theories helped legitimise the idea that teachers can and should develop their own philosophies rather than follow ready-made procedures handed to them by others. The Austrian case study summarises some of Schön's discussion about "reflection-in-action", which involves forming and testing hypotheses in the course of ongoing activity, and "reflection-on-action", which occurs after the event and consists of stepping back to consider alternative interpretations (Altrichter et al., 1993, pp. 7-9). Reflection-in-action is difficult to observe, since it consists of what teachers think while they are teaching. However, the country reports give numerous instances of reflection-on-action.

There is consensus that the quality teacher is a reflective practitioner. The French seminar, for example, specifies that good teachers possess the *"capacité à réfléchir sur ses pratiques, à se remettre en cause, à prendre du recul"* [capacity to reflect on their practice, to keep calling themselves into question, to step back] (Altet, 1993, p. 8). Good teachers may even be a little obsessive, as indicated by this statement from one in New Zealand (Ramsay, 1993, p. 58):

> I'm reflecting all the time, even as I drive home from school – what happened there, where did I go wrong, what can I do? I spend at least an hour a day at different times reflecting. Even when I'm out on school duty I'm always one step ahead in my mind. I reflect in the middle of the night. It seems to be an important time in the middle of the night and ideas toss around in my head and I can come up with some good ideas then.

There are also indications of what prompts teachers to reflect. Dissatisfaction with their own practice is the most commonly described stimulus. For example, teachers at a Swedish secondary school voiced dissatisfaction with their curriculum in social and natural studies. One said, "We are not pleased with our structure..." A colleague concurred, "Social and natural studies are difficult. I believe one thing and do another" (Lander, 1993, p. 62). This discrepancy between belief and practice seems likely to cause further reflection and change. Lander reports also hearing statements of this kind from several teachers of mathematics (p. 90). A cause for much reflection especially among secondary teachers was the dilemma that pupils want teachers to know them personally as individuals, but they lose respect for a teacher who tries to relate to them as a peer. A similar dilemma expressed by some teachers was that they are more effective if they show that they are human beings with feelings, but they must not reveal dislike for particular pupils (pp. 100-102). These are among the issues Swedish teachers were thinking about. In France, secondary teachers were critical of the individualism that prevails among teachers at *lycées*, making it difficult to achieve the teamwork necessary to deal with the current pupil population (Altet, 1993, p. 18).

Since good teachers are always dissatisfied with something, they are constantly on the look-out for new ideas. As a New Zealand teacher remarked, "If you have a good idea in this school, it travels" (Ramsay, 1993, p. 50). High-quality teachers are even open to changing their whole philosophy. An experienced teacher in a US middle school was stimulated by a new principal who arranged for them to attend national workshops on student-centred, active learning. She said, "I totally changed a traditional way of thinking and teaching to one that involves the students so that I don't have to be in front of the classroom anymore. It takes longer to do but it means more to the students" (White and Roesch, 1993, p. 63).

Sometimes a national policy stimulates reflection. The Italian case study provides an example. "In many cases (...) the introduction of the Record of Achievement has required thinking about the link between teaching and learning and also that learning involves cognitive and non-cognitive dimensions" (Macconi, 1993, p. 32).

One goal of current educational reform is for teachers' reflection to become ongoing. The case studies provide examples of that happening. One of the Finnish teachers was reported "to think deeply about his work (...). He appeared to spend time carefully examining the basis of his work and considering ways of putting his ideas into practice (...). This teacher really uses the curriculum as a starting point for his own planning" (Hämäläinen and Jokela, p. 23). In a different school, where teachers have been involved in self-assessment, one teacher said, "We talk about the possibility of doing things in a different way so as to attain even better results. One must really get involved, one has to think" (p. 35). And in another Finnish school (p. 49):

> The willingness of the teachers and the principal to study was evident in many ways. When discussing the various facets of the school, reference was often made to educational thinkers and concepts. Teachers were also very interested in the researchers' reading recommendations. The school did not regard them merely as observers but as consultants who could help develop the school. Attempts have been made to implement those theories taken from educational texts that have been positively valued. For example, the school's method of workshop activity was based on Howard Gardner's theory on the seven types of intelligence.
>
> The school's critical thinking is also revealed in the way they view the curriculum. Officially the curriculum laid down by the municipality (...) is followed. The staff, however, express reservations regarding its superficiality. Consequently, the teachers of the school are continually writing a school-level curriculum. Objectives, contents, means and methods of evaluation are the subjects of continuous development.

A similar spirit of inquiry and continuous improvement is also evident elsewhere. For example, Swedish secondary teachers talked about how they could use the fact of teaching the same subject to several different classes of pupils as an opportunity to try out a range of methods and find out what works best (Almius *et al.*, 1993, p. 31). In the United States, teachers at a middle school experimented with combining special- and general-education students, and carefully monitored the effects (White and Roesch, 1993, pp. 52-53).

In addition to improving practice, reflection also improves communication. As stated by the Austrian seminar, "Teachers reflect on their own actions and are ready to make them transparent to parents and pupils" (Ribolits, 1993, p. 11). Ramsay noted that the teachers he witnessed in New Zealand "all were able to explicate good theories" (p. 55). As communication spreads good ideas and shares understanding, it may contribute to an ongoing cycle of individual reflection, discussion, and continuous improvement.

Collaborate with other teachers

Beyond exchanging ideas and sharing reflection in order to improve their individual practice, many high-quality teachers also participate in teams that plan and teach together. In several of the country studies, this is said to be an increasingly important part of the teacher's role. "*La nécessité pour les enseignants d'aujourd'hui de travailler en équipe*" [the need for today's teachers to work as a team] was the main point to emerge from the survey of teachers conducted by participants in the French seminar, in response to a question about new tasks for teachers (Altet, 1993, p. 20). The capacity for teamwork was also the most frequent response to a question about what constitutes teacher quality at the school level (p. 14). To prepare new teachers to work in teams, the new French University Institutes for Teacher Training are forming teacher trainees into small groups who work and study together (Barbier and Galatanu, 1993, p. 16). Similarly, preparing teachers to participate in collaborative "working units" was one of the reasons for the reorganisation of Swedish teacher education in 1988 (Askling and Jedeskog, 1993, p. 6). Participants in the Swedish seminar noted that collaboration can be an especially valuable experience for new teachers and for those who are not functioning effectively (Almius *et al.*, 1993, pp. 40, 43). In Italy, the Record of Achievement has required teachers at each grade level in the same middle school to plan together for individual students, and has also necessitated that teachers of the same discipline in different schools get together to agree on criteria for evaluating students' performance (Macconi, 1993, pp. 18, 28).

Although central authorities may encourage or even mandate collaboration, it may not always happen to the extent or in the manner desired. For example, Norway's 1987 curriculum guidelines give schools more control over curriculum development. The responsibility is supposed to be shared between teachers and the municipal school authorities (Baasland, 1993, pp. 12-13). However, in one school district with ten schools, only one of them in 1990-91 had met the Municipal Education Committee's deadline for preparing their curricula (p. 34), and in two case-study primary schools the teachers still had only done outlines as of 1993 (pp. 44-45). Similarly, schools in England have been given control over funds for teachers' professional development, but the connection between development plans for individual teachers and the school as a whole was not always clear (Baker *et al.*, 1993, p. 13). These findings reflect not only the possibility that schools may misunderstand or give low priority to central directives, but also the difficulty of achieving effective collaboration among teachers, especially on schoolwide matters. This difficulty is discussed further below.

The country studies of individual schools and teachers provide numerous instances of collaborative efforts, many of them apparently successful in the sense that teachers did work together and felt the process was worthwhile. For example, all except one of the schools studied in New Zealand had established "syndicates" or "development groups" in which teachers collaborated on professional development (Ramsay, 1993, p. 23).

Most of the collaborations described in the country studies were focused on planning and delivering instruction for pupils. The Australian study described schools exploring changes in work organisation with support from the National Schools Project. At one primary school teachers formed three "learning support groups", for years K-2, 3-4, and 5-6. Each group devised new ways of deploying pupils' time with the teachers in the group (McRae, 1993, pp. 20-26). Similarly, another primary school grouped teachers into three "level teams", which planned and sometimes taught together (p. 37). At a Catholic primary school collaboration was already well advanced, with all staff participating in teaching teams. Teachers commented, "you have a fantastic level of support"; "new ideas are coming through all the time"; "I haven't had a bad experience of it"; "people lead you to new resources"; "there is always someone who knows"; "life is a constant in-service". The principal also noted an increase in the level of student activity in classrooms: "Teachers are 'with' their students more, rather than being at the front" (p. 66).

As in the Australian report, teacher collaboration is a major theme in the US case study. Many of the joint efforts are focused on curricular innovations. One teacher wrote about her experience organising a "writing across the curriculum" programme at a middle school. English teachers became advisers to the other departments. Teachers were first given an opportunity to write about themselves, and they responded enthusiastically. The school published a book with the teachers' writings, which attracted attention from outside and fed the enthusiasm. At its peak, four teachers attended a summer workshop of the national Writing Project, and only one of them was an English teacher. "Writing continued in the classroom – many disciplines used journals and writing to learn. Our reluctant writers were producing much more work than ever. Strong narratives and much story telling were being done" (White and Roesch, 1993, p. 56).

Other examples of joint instructional activities in the US study:

A fifth-grade team planned and carried out an ambitious project involving students in producing a play by Aristophanes. Students have made museum visits and then designed and produced Greek costumes, dramatic masks, and a model of a Greek theatre to be modified and built as their stage set. Teachers "put an extraordinary amount of time, energy, and money into the projects" (p. 49).

At a middle school, teachers from several disciplines worked together on a project based on the play *Dragonwings*, about a Chinese immigrant to the US at the turn of the century who is fascinated by flight. The English teacher assigned students to write about immigrants. The science teacher will take up the physics of flight. The math class will be making kites (p. 59).

At another middle school "an eighth-grade team was engaged in what they described as 'pushing the limits' and 'taking risks' in a pilot interdisciplinary unit on change. Students were allowed to sign up for and work on many independent projects in science, social studies, English and math until they had earned 1000 points". Projects dealt with a wide array of topics including the history of language, designing and flying geometric kites, and urban design – including use of the computerised simulation game, *Sim City* (p. 69).

Primary school teachers spend their lunch hour discussing the nature and characteristics of materials appropriate for beginning readers. They bring examples of children's literature from their own classrooms and argue about them, eventually agreeing on a desired sequence and how materials can be made available to different classrooms, though some philosophical differences remain (pp. 42-43).

Sweden, too, offers numerous examples of teachers collaborating on curriculum. Collaboration has increased considerably during the past decade, not only in the case study schools but all over the country, according to Lander (1993, p. 62). He notes that by creating "big thematical projects" teachers also "give their schools a profile". This was not the teachers' original motivation for increased collaboration, but now it also serves this other purpose in response to the recent national policy of allowing parents to choose their children's schools. (This is an example of the phenomenon analysed in the next chapter, of schools harnessing policy initiatives for their own purposes.) Examples from the case-study schools include:

Science teachers at a secondary school together wrote a set of lesson plans which they all use in their grade 9 classes (p. 65).

At the same school, science teachers used their in-service training time to work together on revising the introduction to physics in grade 7. "The idea is to ground physics more firmly by making the concept 'particle' more central (...). By an early introduction of particles, concepts used to describe matter – like 'atom', 'molecule', 'ion', 'element', and so on – will become easier to understand" (p. 94).

A primary school teacher enjoys collaborative curriculum development: "It would be fun if groups within the school could try out different things, write a contract with each other, evaluate it and then report to each other. That would really be training for the whole school. I have used this kind of work at the school where I worked before. I was responsible for three or four projects of that kind, group-work, documenting it, evaluating it, and reporting it. Those were peaks in my professional life. I would like to do so again, but I believe that money is lacking. During the 80s there was state money to apply for" (p. 141).

In several primary schools, teachers collectively implemented "non-graded" classes, *i.e.* combining pupils in grades 1-3. In part this was a response to the fact that new pupils each year were becoming "harder to socialise and train for"; teachers "did not want to be left alone with the beginners one more time" (p. 151). In addition, non-grading was seen as "a good instrument for more co-operation among teachers and thereby for better instruction" (p. 156).

Teachers in Finnish schools also collaborate on curriculum and instruction. In one school, a 1992 questionnaire found that 74 per cent of the teachers collaborated with each other at least on a weekly basis. The collaboration among second-grade teachers was "especially close and well organised. [It] involves not only common planning but also taking advantage of one another's strengths, participating in common projects and entering into flexible substitute-teacher arrangements". The groups meets every Friday afternoon to plan for the following week. Each week usually has a theme based on the school curriculum. During the week, "pupils may move from one group to another and groups may occasionally be combined. Lesson materials may be exchanged and teachers may advise one another on the use of such material" (Hämäläinen and Jokela, 1993, pp. 42-43).

Although there are many examples of teachers working together, collaboration can be difficult and sometimes impossible because of differences in personality or philosophy. The Swedish seminar produced examples (Lander and Odhagen, p. 15):

> The staff of the English department cannot agree about how to improve work. Of the five teachers, three are interested in developmental work, one is irresolute but is "controlled" by the will of the fifth, who is totally against any changes. In spite of several attempts to find compromises she completely refuses to co-operate.

> Teachers in science and social studies have planned to work with projects about environmental problems (...). But (...) enthusiasm fades away in front of most science teachers' unsympathetic attitude. Projects' thematical organisation is considered "lousy" ideas. The principal notices what is going on but does not react.

The school's biggest problem is said to be lack of collaboration within subject departments. Colleagues do not want to tell each other about their working methods and do not want to engage in joint tasks to improve instruction.

Four teachers in mathematics are working with different ability groups across classes. One of them refuses to take part in a solution worked out by the others. The organisation and pupils' free choice demand a common organisation. Should the refusing teacher be voted down, or not?

Ironing out such conflicts takes time, energy, and sometimes outside resources. At the Finnish school where the smooth collaboration among teachers was described above, "conscious attempts to improve the school's atmosphere (...) have included many occasions on which the aim has been to alleviate tensions between the staff members. An outside psychologist has provided assistance during a number of meetings regarding possible areas in which staff relationships may be developed (...). Such discussions have drawn attention to the fact that nothing is achieved through mere accusation and that compromises must be reached by the disputing parties" (Hämäläinen and Jokela, 1993, p. 39).

Collaboration becomes still more difficult when it departs from immediate matters of curriculum and instruction in the participants' own classrooms and enters the strategic realm of schoolwide policy and planning. White and Roesch (1993, p. 86) tally the risks to teachers who take on this broader task:

At each of these schools, a critical mass of teachers who had previously been working individually (...) decided to try working collaboratively to develop a schoolwide approach to identifying and solving problems. These teachers risk investing relatively large amounts of time and energy with very little guaranteed return. In developing a common vision, they risk having their most cherished beliefs and philosophies open for challenge, negotiation, or rejection. They risk the discomfort of interacting with peers, some of whom they were not sure they could work with (...). They risk giving up their autonomy and the relative ease of making changes within the privacy of their own classrooms. In many cases they risk losing the status and decision-making power they had already earned in the current school hierarchical organisation. These teachers also risk opposition from parents and/or the central administration who might oppose the dropping of practices that currently enjoy popular support.

Appended to the United States report are essays by two teachers who took these risks and participated actively in school development efforts. Entitled "Journey of a Sceptic" and "Learning a New Dance", these essays eloquently describe the doubts, frustrations, endless meetings over periods of several years, and finally the rewards of achieving commitment to shared goals.

Lander analysed Swedish teachers' perceptions of their own collective "strategic capacity". This was measured by the extent of agreement with the following statements: "Teachers are good at driving improvements of the school work", and "Teachers are good at systematically planning and making improvements happen in our daily work". Secondary, but not primary, teachers were also asked to what extent they agreed that: "In our subject department we are good at putting up shared ambitions to direct our school work", "In our working unit we are good at putting up shared ambitions to direct our work", and "At conferences all teachers take interest in discussing the common issues of the school work" (Lander, 1993, Appendix 5.2).

Regression analysis of responses for primary and secondary teachers separately found only one predictor other than pupil background factors that was significantly associated with perceived strategic capacity at both primary and secondary levels (Appendix 5.4). This was a variable measuring the frequency of "strategic discussions" about pupil evaluation criteria and school goals. One interpretation of this result is that having more meetings to discuss strategic issues contributes to teachers' sense of their own strategic capacity. Another interpretation is that it is easier to have meetings to discuss strategic issues if teachers are already confident of their strategic capacity. Both interpretations may be true.

More generally, teachers' individual commitment to their work also may tend to be stronger in schools where there is more collaboration. An Austrian teacher at an academic secondary school explains: "For instance, when I approach a colleague and ask him, 'Would you like to do some project work with me?', there is not much fussing around but he will say either yes or no. And normally you're not given a refusal. In my previous school these things have certainly happened: I wanted to get a project going and I was met with a rebuff. It was too much work for the colleagues. In this school the staff is very active, they want to work, and this is supported by the fact that they are competent to do so" (Altrichter *et al.*, 1993, pp. 39-40). Collaboration and commitment can be mutually enhancing.

Advance the profession of teaching

Beyond their own classrooms and schools, high-quality teachers also assume responsibility for contributing to the knowledge base of the teaching profession. But as these teachers become more active and visible, a problem arises: how to keep them in the classroom? The country reports had a number of things to say about developing the teaching profession.

Several countries offered examples of teachers involved in building the knowledge base. In the United States (White and Roesch, 1993, p. 91):

Teachers and administrators at each of the schools studied read, quote, share, and use the latest research from national journals, books and workshops on topics ranging from site-based management to whole-language teaching to student portfolio assessments. They also write and present nationally what they have learned from their local experiences. In 1993 their publications ranged from an article in *Educational Leadership*; to presentations at national, state, and county conferences; to articles in state and local newspapers, to publication in county and school-based journals.

One of the schools studied in Finland is associated with a university, and therefore is especially involved in research. "Research projects form an integral part of the teacher's daily work. In addition to this, each teacher is granted a 'sabbatical' every seventh year" to focus on a research problem. "Through research the teacher develops both himself and his work. Moreover, the results of the research have a wider use (...). Many of the school's teachers have also played an active part in producing new study materials" for national in-service training courses (Hämäläinen and Jokela, 1993, p. 22). Although this degree of involvement in research is not typical of other schools in Finland (or elsewhere), the national goals for teacher education in Finland include preparing every new teacher "to identify, analyse and solve (...) scientific and professional problems in his or her own field (...) [and] to promote the development of his/her own professional sector and to continuously acquire new scientific information necessary in his/her field" (quoted in Buchberger et al., 1990a, p. 3).

Numerous examples have already been given of teachers trying something new and observing the results. The more this is done in a replicable manner, the more it approaches research in the conventional academic sense. For instance, teachers at an upper secondary school in Australia initiated field trials of several new ideas, including early entry of gifted students from feeder schools, developing a "fully integrated, multimedia information kiosk" in the field of small business management, a learning assistance programme using computerised assessment, and an early exit programme allowing advanced students to graduate early (McRae, 1993, pp. 52-56). Whether or not such initiatives succeed, the results might be of interest to other schools if teachers published them. Altrichter et al. would like Austrian teachers and schools to learn from others' experience as well as from their own (p. 38), and they propose that teachers publish accounts of their own school development efforts so that others might learn from them (p. 44).

Building the knowledge base could help improve the status of the teaching profession. Teachers in some countries feel they do not receive enough recognition for what they do. For example, this came through loud and clear in the French seminar, where teachers felt that improving teacher quality was linked to greater social recognition of teachers, *"une revalorisation de la profession enseignante"* [a re-valuation of the teaching profession] (Altet, 1993, pp. 16, 38).

A related problem discussed in some of the reports is that the best teachers sometimes leave the teaching profession to become administrators. The New Zealand seminar registered "concern that the standard career path of the quality teacher was promotion out of the classroom into the field of administration. Alternative career paths need to be established to enable the quality teacher who wishes to teach (...) to be able to do so without any adverse remunerative impact" (New Zealand Ministry of Education, 1993, p. 39). Suggestions included creating positions for master or lead teachers, arranging for lateral transfers to other schools or colleges of education, and providing sabbaticals (pp. 51, 62).

Japan provides a certain amount of allocation of co-ordinating and guiding roles within the teaching profession by giving some senior teachers the title of *shunin* with responsibility for academic affairs, pupils' health or guidance, the schools' clerical work, or affairs of a single grade-level (Maki, 1992, p. 2). Macconi (1993, p. 35) notes that teachers also have organisational tasks within Italian schools, such as being in charge of affairs for a single grade-level, chairing a committee, or being deputy head. Especially if they carry extra compensation, these titles may satisfy some teachers' desire for individual advancement. By retaining quality teachers, this differentiation of roles may also help advance the profession as a whole.

Although the case studies and seminars talk about adding to the profession's knowledge base and upgrading the status of teachers, they are silent about membership in unions or professional organisations. This was not identified as a particular topic for inquiry in the design of the case studies and seminars. Presumably some, conceivably all, of the teachers in these studies belonged to unions or professional groups, but their participation is not described.

Contribute to society at large

Highly accomplished teachers sometimes see their professional responsibility extending beyond the educational system itself to encompass broader social concerns. They design their instruction to help students come to grips with social problems and conflicts.

An example is the multicultural curriculum unit on immigration created by a group of teachers at one of the middle schools studied in the United States (White and Roesch, 1993, pp. 61-63). Students in history classes researched their own cultural heritage by interviewing family members, constructing family trees, and interviewing immigrants who were not members of their own families. A class for gifted and talented students wrote short stories based on interviews with immigrants; one of these earned third prize in a national contest. Students also read books about their own ethnic backgrounds, and they made short oral presentations in which they shared pictures, artefacts, music, language, or vignettes. A Moslem girl from Pakistan answered questions about observance of Ramadan, and about arranged marriages. A Vietnamese boy "talked about his family and proudly served rice dumplings from his mother's Vietnamese restaurant" (p. 62). A Canadian immigrant who played in a championship hockey team was described by his great granddaughter. The daughter of a Scottish immigrant brought bagpipes and pictures of her father's clan. A boy from Bolivia told about his life and brought artefacts to show the class. Some of the teachers also described their own immigrant forebearers. A teacher, in fact, set an example for the students by being the first to make a presentation. By creating a positive atmosphere, teachers helped students see ethnic differences as something to honour, even celebrate. In addition to increasing students' knowledge about their own histories and those of their classmates, this lesson seemed to stimulate genuine interest in one another's origins. Quite consciously, these teachers are trying to improve the cohesion of their increasingly multicultural society.

The French seminar raised a similar issue. Teachers are responsible for fulfilling the national commitment to enable 80 per cent of students to achieve the *baccalauréat* (Altet, 1993, p. 2). At all levels, they are faced with students who are more heterogeneous and less selected than before. However, participants in the seminar thought that only a minority of teachers so far have actively embraced their new responsibility (pp. 37-38). Altrichter *et al.* also note that teachers in the schools they studied did not identify strongly with national education authorities, and they express concern that this "mental uncoupling" may impede the effectiveness of education as a social instrument (pp. 35-36).

It seems that teachers who do take responsibility for dealing with social issues are often not responding directly to administrative mandates. Instead, they are motivated by their own concerns and those of their colleagues and school community. Central policies may, in fact, help orient teachers toward local concerns, as in Norway, where school decentralisation, participation of teachers on school planning committees, and in-service training in school management seem to have had this effect. The case-study report observes, "The managements of the three schools have developed an understanding of the school as an important institution in society. The leaders have educational skills and the ability to combine educational questions with the demands, needs and wishes of the local community. They are interested in developing the schools into institutions functioning in the local community" (Baasland, 1993, p. 44).

One of the most fundamental contributions teachers make to solving social problems is helping their pupils become clear thinkers. A New Zealand teacher explains (Ramsay, 1993, p. 47):

> My classroom is based on research and problem solving. I'm seeking to develop individual learners who are self-starters and completers. I constantly challenge children to find possible solutions. I seldom tell them what it is that I want, although on occasions, to get progress, I will do some direct teaching. I follow the children's initiatives. I will extend the time on an activity if it seems profitable and the children's interest is being held. Capturing the child's curiosity is essential. I encourage them to think, how to reconstruct problems. They have lots of knowledge themselves and I bring that to bear by introducing new knowledge and seeing if we can find a best way to solve a problem. I'm looking all the time for valid learning experiences and I know, because the children and parents tell me, that I use "why" an awful lot in my classroom teaching.

Learning to ask "why" is vital for responsible citizens.

Conclusion

To recapitulate, the country studies depict the world of teachers as inreasingly complex and changing. A tenacious commitment to helping students learn makes good teachers keep trying to improve, even when the work is difficult and demoralising. They must keep up with changing conceptions of their subject matter, and continually add to their repertory of instructional methods. Creating the necessary rapport with students is a fresh challenge with each new class, especially when there are more students who come from other countries or who lack family support. Simply growing older requires learning new ways to relate to students. Increasingly, teachers are diversifying their pedagogical strategies to incorporate pupil-centered and small-group techniques, which are more consistent with contemporary theories of human learning and also more appealing to students who prefer interactive learning. Computers and other digitised-information technologies are also becoming more important tools for teaching and learning, finally changing the ancient method of chalk and talk. The complex interactions of personalities and pedagogies make classroom dynamics increasingly unpredictable, and teachers must be adept at improvisation. As there is more to think about, reflection has come to be an expected part of teachers' work, and good teachers may even become somewhat obsessed, working on weekends and waking in the night with ideas for their classrooms. Exchanging ideas and support with colleagues has become increasingly vital. In addition to informal exchanges, teachers participate in formal conferences and workshops, contributing to the professional knowledge base. Collaboration among teachers is also increasingly being required, as teachers in many schools are given additional responsibility for planning curriculum and instruction, managing resources, and organising their own professional development programmes.

The country studies give us a picture of highly accomplished teachers as exceptionally intelligent, dedicated individuals who, when they think about it, tend to feel they do not receive recognition or compensation commensurate with their efforts and accomplishments. This is not a new image; it is even somewhat stereotypical. And, in the early 1990s, perhaps teachers were not alone in feeling overworked and underpaid. Nevertheless, this chapter has confirmed the hypothesis advanced in the first two chapters: that changes in education and society are placing new demands on teachers. Yet, despite widespread discussion of the necessity to improve salaries and working conditions in order to attract and retain teachers who can do all this well, salaries and working conditions have not yet dramatically improved. And the fact that the problem is widely recognised may make it more difficult for teachers themselves to put it out of their minds.

What, then, prevents talented teachers from quitting in large numbers and finding work that offers them greater compensation and recognition? Love of children and commitment to helping them learn seem to be important motivations to continue in teaching. The support of colleagues in the working environment is vital to maintaining motivation, as this chapter has shown. Chapter 6 analyses the nature of these supportive local environments. The local school context also mediates the effects of central policies, to be described now in the next chapter.

Chapter 5

Policies Described in the Country Studies

This chapter describes the range of policies affecting teacher quality that were considered in the various country studies. It does not attempt to identify the correct policy, nor to evaluate those that were promulgated. The case studies were not designed to evaluate policies, nor to describe the full range of policies that may affect teacher quality. However, the country studies do provide some evidence about the implementation of policies in particular schools and classrooms.

Implementation of policy in education is notoriously complicated, as abundant research has shown. A useful summary has recently been provided by Milbrey McLaughlin (1990) in her re-analysis of the large-scale Rand "Change Agent" study undertaken in the United States in the seventies. She found that many of the conclusions from the study still hold true today, and commented (p. 12) that:

A general finding of the Change Agent study that has become almost a truism is that it is exceedingly difficult for policy to change practice, especially across levels of government. Contrary to the one-to-one relationship assumed to exist between policy and practice, the Change Agent study demonstrated that the nature, amount, and pace of change at the local level was a product of local factors that were largely beyond the control of higher-level policy makers.

According to McLaughlin, this general observation has three specific implications:

– policy cannot mandate what matters to people in schools;
– implementation dominates outcomes;
– local variability is the rule; uniformity is the exception.

McLaughlin also described those strategies that were effective in promoting educational improvement, especially when used together:

– concrete, teacher-specific and extended training;
– classroom assistance from local staff;
– teacher observation of similar projects in other classrooms, schools or districts;
– regular project meetings that focus on practical issues;
– teacher participation in project decisions;
– local development of project materials;
– principal's or head's participation in training.

In short, although policies set directions and provide a framework, they do not and cannot determine outcomes. It is implementation, rather than the decision to adopt a new policy, that determines student achievement. This theme will be taken up again in the next chapter.

The rest of this chapter is organised around four of the key policy themes from the country studies: pre-service teacher education, in-service teacher education and staff development, teacher performance appraisal, and devolution of increased responsibility to individual schools. We note, however, that some of the policies described in the case studies do not fit neatly into these four categories. In Italy, for example, the main topic of the case study was the implementation of the new Record of Achievement for pupils in middle school. Although there was a substantial amount of in-service teacher education in support of the policy, the effects on teacher quality also gave teachers a collective responsibility for pupil assessment, and stimulated much discussion among teachers about theory and practice.

Pre-service teacher education

The country reports indicate that the policies developed and implemented to improve the initial preparation of teachers are, by and large, comprehensive in scope and have major implications for all involved. They include policies to recruit better candidates, upgrade the content or position of teacher training, monitor programmes more closely, update teacher educators, and improve practice teaching.

Promote the recruitment of high-quality candidates into teaching. Reports in several countries have commented unfavourably on the quality of candidates admitted to teacher education programmes. Typically, the criterion used in the selection of students into teacher education is academic ability. Clearly, there is competition from more prestigious and well-paying professions. There are variations on this theme in some countries where local cultural and/or contextual factors operate to promote teaching as a career.

Some of the policy initiatives adopted in this area relate to offering entry to students from older age-groups with particular skills and to the provision of teaching scholarships for those students who might not be able to attend if they did not have the financial support during the course and the strong likelihood of a position on completion. There is emerging a framework for "taster" courses to attract mature graduates to switch careers into teaching, along with schemes such as Articled Teacher and Licensed Teacher.

Change the location of teacher education programmes. Teacher education is now generally located in the university sector. However, the resulting outcomes for teacher educators and teacher education often do not match those of other professions, *e.g.* medicine. While the movement brought an initial rise in status for teacher education and teacher educators, the increasing emphasis on knowledge generation, *i.e.* research rather than knowledge transmission, has resulted in a relatively weak professional standing in many universities.

In common with the picture in several other countries the Swedish team (Askling and Jedeskog, 1993) report:

> There is a large group of subject teachers, who give many lessons in teacher education and to teacher students' classes, but who do not regard themselves as teacher educators. Their affiliation is to departments where most teaching and almost all research is directed towards academic issues. They mostly identify themselves as university teachers and are sometimes rather reluctant to adopt proposals for more didactical elements in the courses.

This issue can be seen also within schools of education. Here teacher educators concerned with the supervision of practice teaching, for example, often have less status and power than academic staff who can demonstrate that their field has a scientific research base or theoretical frameworks.

France has recently implemented a major initiative involving the establishment of new university teacher training institutes (IUFM). These institutions are notable for three aspects: they move teacher education into the university sector, they introduce research, and they have a degree of relative autonomy which makes it possible to take into account local conditions (Barbier and Galatanu, 1993).

Two general trends were identified in the three particular IUFMs that were studied. One trend was integration of teacher training into the university environment (*universitarisation*). The other was the linking of teacher training to professional practice (*professionalisation*). The different articulation of these two tendencies in the specific training arrangements – the professional paper required of all students, the organisation of practice teaching, the relation between academic and practical courses – determined the different dynamics of progress in the three different institutions.

Although the three IUFMs differed, they all offered two-year programmes containing the similar elements of academic content knowledge, educational theory and teaching strategies, and a practical component. The practical work is guided by one of three types of trainer, depending on the experience of the student teacher. For example, there are "welcoming professors" who are responsible for the first-year high school student teachers, "pedagogical advisor teachers" who are involved with the second-year high school student teachers, and the "master primary education teacher" who works with the primary education students. To become a "field trainer" is a competitive process and those selected have to complete a training programme.

Specify the content of teacher education programmes. Numerous reviews have been conducted of the curriculum of teacher education. In the reports it is possible to discern two possible competing approaches. The first is that there has been a tendency to emphasise academic content at the expense of a more professional and practical pedagogical orientation (Department of Employment, Education and Training, Australia, 1992). The second echoes the work of the Holmes Group (1986), which asserted the importance of "a body of specialised knowledge on teaching, codified and transmitted through professionalisation of teacher education and to teaching".

In some countries it is now possible to see more direct control of initial teacher education course content. In Scotland, for example, all courses of training are subject to the Secretary of State's Guidelines for Courses of Initial Teacher Training (of which a revised version was published in January 1993). Like many others these Guidelines lay down general principles which courses should follow. In addition, every teacher training course has to be approved by the Secretary of State and these Guidelines are used by the Scottish Office of Education in carrying out this process. Recently more emphasis has been put on specific competencies which beginning teachers should possess (Scottish Education Department, 1992).

In Australia there has been a growing concern expressed by the Commonwealth Government at the quality of all aspects of initial teacher education. It is not surprising, therefore, that the Department of Employment, Education and Training (DEET) stated in 1992:

> The last few years have witnessed a heightened public awareness of the importance of teachers and good teaching to the achievement of broad social aims. Addressing and resolving critical issues in teacher education is a central part of a positive response to community demand. Because of the magnitude of its investment in teacher education and its leading role in economic, social and educational matters the Commonwealth believes action is needed.

The DEET outlined what it called "suggestions for action". One initiative was the establishment of the National Project on Quality Teaching and Learning (NPQTL) to consider "ways of improving both initial and ongoing in-service teacher education and considering the potential benefits of national competency-based standards for the teaching profession". The NPQTL was concluded at the end of 1993, although its initiatives in relation to teacher competencies will be continued through another body. A newly established Australian Teaching Council will promote the professional interests of teachers, including the areas of initial and in-service teacher training.

The Commonwealth has argued that the development of national competency standards is a means of making explicit, both within and without the profession, what competent professionals need to know and be able to do, and establishing agreed standards and making them public. Five broad areas of competence have been outlined: teaching practice, student needs, relationships, evaluating and planning, and professional responsibilities. In each of these broad areas a number of elements were distinguished and to help in their understanding a brief case summary of a teacher exhibiting the competence and a set of generic competence criteria were developed.

In Japan a series of reports of the National Council on Educational Reform culminated in 1987 with the recommendation that the content of professional teacher education courses should be reviewed along with the whole organisation and structure of the practice teaching component. The Council made a number of suggestions regarding the content of the initial teacher education course and these have been elaborated by the Teacher Education Council who advised the Minister of Education, Science and Culture accordingly (Maki, 1992*a*).

The country report from Finland (Buchberger, *et al.*, 1993) indicates a focus on "humanistic teacher education" in which students are required to demonstrate knowledge, skills and a professional attitude. There is a national framework for teacher education programmes in Finland and its goals, objectives and structure provide the basis for the programmes. Even so, there is the opportunity for mismatches to occur as emerging classroom needs are always likely to be ahead of course offerings at the university. For example, a sample of recently graduated teachers said they needed more information and practice with technology, multicultural education, and alternative pedagogy (p. 28).

In situations where there is no direct control of content in teacher education it is possible to see how other policy decisions mediate an impact on teacher education. For example, when student profiles and national records of achievement or national curricula are mandated by ministries of education, this decision has a major influence on the content and operation of the teacher education course.

Increase the length of initial teacher preparation courses. In general the teaching force of all countries now has higher formal qualifications than a decade ago. Typically, teacher education programmes require a minimum of one year following the award of a *baccalauréat* degree, or a minimum of three years for a diploma or degree for early years and primary teaching.

Proponents such as the Holmes Group have argued that an extended programme is essential to the professionalisation of teaching. In Australia the Commonwealth Tertiary Education Commission (CTEC) reported in 1986 that there was general professional support for four-year pre-service courses for primary and early childhood teachers. The Committee rejected it, however, on a simple cost-benefits examination. They asserted "there is no significant research evidence to suggest that primary and early childhood teachers would be better suited to cope with the demands of the classroom in the early years of their teaching than are those with three years of training" (CTEC, 1986, p. 51).

Exercise more governance and quality control in teacher education. This issue, in part, is related to the content of teacher education (see above). In many countries there is clearly a move by central government to take direct control of both content and the quality of teacher education programmes. In other countries the content of the initial teacher education programme is negotiated between the institutions, the profession, employing authorities, and state or national co-ordinating authorities.

In general it is now possible to see an increased effort on the part of non-institutional bodies in monitoring teacher education. For example, the large majority of States in the United States require pre-service teachers to pass some specified examination as part of their preparation. This situation is similar to that in Germany where the *Zweites Staatsexanon* must be passed before tenure is granted. Other countries have established registration boards, where standards of professional competence and practice are monitored and applied to graduates seeking employment as teachers.

However, in some countries with a centralised tradition there are reports of movement toward less centralised control. The Austrian country report (Buchberger *et al.*, 1993*a*, p. 1) describes the tradition there:

> As decisions concerning the organisation and structure of initial teacher education in all its aspects (institutions, duration of courses, course structures, exam regulations, certificates) are taken by the central government (Ministry of Education and the Arts, Ministry of Science and Research) all institutions of teacher education in Austria and their programmes are fairly similar in structure.

The Austrian Ministry's involvement is not only related to the content and syllabus of the course. The appointments to the teacher education institutions are made by the Minister of Education on the basis of advice in which the college only has a consultative role (p. 5). It is interesting, therefore, to note that the country report states (p. 19):

> The programme also seems to be exploring ways of changing the traditional culture of teacher education in Austria, which has been controlled in terms of national curricula and principles of teaching for teacher education.
>
> In the new, emerging culture more emphasis is being placed on individual responsibility and co-operation, working towards a learning community. This is clearly a significant shift towards a collaborative culture in teacher education.

Change the teacher educators. There are numerous reports which point to the gap between the perceived needs of the beginning teacher and what is provided in the initial preparation course. Often it is said that the gap exists because the teacher educators have not kept pace with the changes in curricula, teaching strategies, and so on.

In some countries this has resulted in policies which either place more responsibility for the pre-service work in schools or requires teacher educators to have "recent and relevant" school experience. For example, in Scotland the large majority of teacher educators are former school teachers. They are required by law to be registered, like teachers, with the General Teaching Council for Scotland. Another consequence has been the significant increase in the numbers of teachers seconded from schools for limited periods.

Faculty members in the new French IUFMs were observed to be taking on new functions: advising students writing their professional papers, leading groups of student teachers in seminars, and supervising practice teaching. Through these new activities, the faculty members were evolving a new professional identity for themselves, with a triple competence as teachers of their own subjects, as trainers of student teachers, and as researchers (Barbier and Galatanu, 1993).

Improve the practical experience of students. Many reports referred to the need to provide beginning teachers with better structured and articulated field experiences in schools. It was often noted that student teachers at present do not have the opportunity to acquire a repertoire of teaching strategies and skills which contribute to being an effective practitioner.

In some countries the approach is to immerse student teachers in a whole-school environment where they focus on the school rather than the university for the practical pedagogy needed to be successful. For example, Scotland announced certain measures to reform teacher training (Scottish Education Department, 1992). A new set of guidelines issued in January 1993 to the teacher training institutions placed more stress than hitherto on the competences which a new teacher should display when entering the profession. The amount of time to be spent by students in schools during their training was to be extended to ensure that training was more closely related to the job which the students would be doing once they qualified. The new guidelines announced extension of school experience in all courses except the PGCE primary, where the difficulty of ensuring in the short time available that students could cover the curriculum of the primary school has meant a postponement of a decision to extend school experience in that course (p. 5).

In England and Wales (Baker *et al.*, 1993) a similar picture is evident. As described in this country report, "the content of ITT [initial teacher training] is defined by the competences that trainees are expected to achieve" (p. 5). To achieve these competences, there is increasing reliance on practice teaching in schools.

In other countries there is emerging discussion on the need to establish professional development schools. It is argued these will promote school-university partnerships ranging from the preparation of novice teachers, through ongoing professional development of experienced teachers, to the research and development work required by the profession. It is, as the Holmes Group (1990) assert, where "the schools management, leadership, and faculty – including colleagues from the University [must] work together to invent a new organisational structure in line with the school's new purposes and principles about teaching and learning" (p. 67). This concept is gaining support from a variety of participants – teachers, administrators, university staff, policy makers, etc. – but the problems of implementation have not all been addressed.

A further aspect which is receiving attention is the selection of co-operating teachers, *i.e.* the practising teachers who assist the student teachers when they first begin their supervised teaching. In some countries this is a fairly haphazard process whereby the institutions seek teachers willing to take on this role. In other countries the process for becoming a co-operating teacher is prescribed by the relevant State ministry of education. The selection criteria involve both interviews with the applicant and a series of observed demonstration lessons.

In summary, over the last decade there has been a continuous programme of radical education reform. At the heart of this has been policy makers' concerns with perceived inadequacies and omissions in teacher education. It is interesting to observe that in relation to teaching and school teachers the trend appears to be away from top-down or centralised initiatives to approaches which increase teachers' autonomy and authority over their work. On the other hand, in many issues relating to initial teacher preparation it is possible to see more government or centralised control. The outcomes of this action will be seen in the future. The various country reports, however, lead to a sense of optimism. There are many examples which show that teacher educators and administrators recognise and seek involvement in a process of ongoing change in the philosophy, content and presentation of teacher education courses. The balance needs to be maintained between external initiatives which will limit their autonomy and flexibility and their need for self- and professional recognition.

In-service teacher education and staff development

The country reports show that school systems are now active in in-service teacher education (INSET) programmes. This is a relatively new activity and can be dated from the introduction of new curricula in the 1960s and 1970s (Lieberman and Miller, 1978). Prior to this there was little official understanding that the implementation of any innovation required training for the people who were going to use it.

In contrast to the movement in some countries toward more centralised control of pre-service teacher education, the general trend in INSET seems to be toward decentralisation, as INSET is used to support school-based decision-making and programme improvement. Some countries still retain centralised control over INSET but take local preferences into account. In Italy, for example (Macconi, 1993, p. 5):

> In order to avoid the excessive fragmentation of initiatives and to achieve a better use of resources, each year a national in-service plan is defined and implemented on the national, provincial and local levels, always taking as its starting point the needs expressed by the teaching staff of individual schools.

Japan appears to be similar (Maki, 1992a). The Japanese are concerned to make clear the responsibilities of the national, prefectural and municipal governments for in-service education and how the courses can be incorporated into a whole. The Japanese, like others, are mandating in-service education (p. 3):

> The periodical programmes will allow teachers to reflect on their own teaching experiences, acquire new professional knowledge, revitalise themselves and further improve their own capacity for classroom and other activities.

The Norwegian country report (Baasland, 1993) describes how the central authorities have given priority to changes in curricula, teaching strategies, and social equity. The school and the region have the responsibility for ensuring that these issues are addressed.

In other countries, control over INSET has been decentralised as part of the policy to place more decision-making responsibility at the local school level. The Finnish case study provides a very good illustration of this (Hämäläinen and Jokela, 1993). In 1994, new curricula are planned for Finland, as is an increased level of autonomy for schools (p. 5):

> This dismantling of management structures (revising rules which control the independent functioning of teachers, schools and municipalities) is to encourage individual schools and *teachers to plan, put into practice and evaluate their functioning more independently and more flexibly than before* [emphasis in original].

To successfully move to these new modes of teacher thinking and behaviour an intensive in-service programme is necessary.

In Sweden there was a similar picture but it is now slightly different. In the 1980s teachers had approximately five study-days per year. These were locally organised and paid for, but the national authorities usually decided the specific content for one or more days. There were provided national and municipal grants in agreed proportions for local school initiatives, and national grants for in-service training courses at the universities.

These frameworks were amended in 1990 (Lander, personal correspondence, 26th January, 1994):

> Study days were increased to 24 over a three-year period; however, there are now no state grants earmarked for school development and in-service training. In fact, municipalities are expected to buy in-service training and other expert help for school development in the market place. In sum, it can be said that there is not much left of the former state support system for school development and in-service training, at least when we are talking about its administrative structure.

Money allocation is to a very high extent under municipal power. But time allocation was definitely changed due to national decisions when the time for study-days was increased by more than 50 per cent. The underlying premise for today's decentralised structure is that in-service training and school development are the tools of the local organisation. What is still left of central state influence is that teacher colleges and teacher training departments at universities, by far the dominant providers of teacher training, are paid with state money – not for in-service training, which is bought on the market by schools and municipalities, but for pre-service training of teachers. This is the basic foundation of innovativeness, and the testing out of ideas, for in-service training also.

The issue of commercialisation of in-service activities, and professional development in general is referred to in the England and Wales report. Baker *et al.* (1993, p. 7) note:

> Several LEAs have responded by putting their professional development functions on a more commercial footing. Some have introduced incentives to encourage LEA-maintained schools to continue to use their services. However a range of other providers is gradually emerging and it will be for schools to identify those offering the services most appropriate to their needs and circumstances.

One consequence of this move has been a much closer monitoring of in-service courses and, in some instances, evaluation of the training as a condition for allocating funds. Unfortunately, however, evaluation and monitoring themselves require time and resources. "Schools felt that formal evaluation took more time than they had available; in one school, crowded agendas for general staff meetings had resulted in professional development receiving little attention at all" (p. 22).

Teachers in these country studies reportedly like INSET. The Austrian case study found, "in-service training provisions are – out of all support offered from the system (*i.e.* national and regional administration and inspectorate) – most highly valued by our interviewees" (Altrichter *et al.*, 1993, p. 21). Similarly, participants in the New Zealand teacher seminar (New Zealand Ministry of Education, 1993, p. 25) saw INSET as essential:

> Initial teacher training and education was seen as being quite inadequate to secure the teacher for their entire career. Because knowledge grows exponentially, because curricula are constantly evolving, because research on the teaching/learning process continues to reveal new insights and because epistemologies and methodologies change, it is imperative that teachers keep abreast of such developments and translate them into quality practice.

However, there is some danger that commercialisation of professional development programmes may lead to a parade of disconnected workshops rather than supporting a serious investment in teachers' own study of their work. Lander (1993) points out that providers of in-service training must have insights into school improvement processes, and the skills of intervening with them. This entails the capacity to co-operate with, and assist, the schools in arranging for learning within the regular setting, as a necessary complement of the INSET course or workshop. Providers from teacher colleges and universities in Sweden are slowly learning how to address this topic, but much more change is needed. If evaluation of INSET does not include long-term effects on teachers and schools, it may not prevent programmatic fragmentation.

Teacher performance appraisal

There are indications in the country studies that teacher appraisal or evaluation is growing in importance. Often it is linked to wider staff development considerations, but appraisal varies among countries in focus, breadth and place in a total framework.

In the United States, the case study of schools in Fairfax County includes a description of the countrywide system for appraising teachers, using eight criteria: Teachers should demonstrate a knowledge of content and curriculum; provide appropriate learning experience; demonstrate appropriate planning; manage instruction and behaviour of students; demonstrate human relations and communication skills; monitor and evaluate student and programme outcomes; use available resources; fulfil professional responsibilities (White and Roesch, 1993, pp. 13-14).

This list is for the most part congruent with the description of quality teaching in Chapter 5, but here there is no explicit mention of reflection or of teacher collaboration. Performance in these eight dimensions is considered in a three-step progression from Entry Level to Career Level 1 and Career Level 2, and teachers are appraised on a four-point scale: exemplary, skilful, marginal and ineffective. Teachers whose performance has been rated "marginal" will be referred to the intervention programme, and those who are rated ineffective are recommended for termination of employment.

The Scottish report (Scottish Education Department, 1992) outlines a very comprehensive approach which is predicated on the assertion that "Staff development has to be approached in a systematic way to be successful" (p. 6). In 1989 the Secretary of State in a consultation paper entitled "School teachers' Professional Development into the 1990s", suggested that there should be National Guidelines for Staff Development and Appraisal, with appraisal being defined as the assessment of the performance of individual teachers (*ibid.*). The Guidelines are designed to ensure a planned and systematic approach to staff development and appraisal and a degree of consistency across the country. The approach adopted recognises that there are a number of purposes that can be seen in an individual appraisal system operating within the broader context of staff development. These are:

- Motivation and communication, including the opportunity to discuss the aims and objectives of current school policies and practices and to influence future developments.
- Review, evaluation and development of professional performance, including formal evaluation of all aspects of an individual's contribution to the team. Managers explore how performance in some aspect of the individual's work could be enhanced and what steps could help achieve this.
- Identification of personal staff development needs, providing an opportunity to identify personal development needs and to discuss how they can be met.
- Career review, giving advice and support in relation to career development. It both indicates suitability for future promotion and identifies performance below acceptable standards.

It is important to note that appraisal is not seen as replacing existing procedures for promotion or dealing with unsatisfactory performance. Other policies relate to these procedures. The policy, in essence, is targeted, but flexible enough to cater for local circumstances, *i.e.* it says "teachers ought to be involved in designing the arrangement, both at school and authority level".

England has a similar scheme to Scotland. But the case study (Baker *et al.* 1993) found that the linking of the various systems – appraisal and the School Development Plans – was not yet completed in the case study schools.

In New Zealand, as part of the requirement that each school has a School Charter (similar to the School Development Plans in the United Kingdom), it was reported by Ramsay (1993) that many schools have sophisticated systems of teacher appraisal and development in place. In these examples, appraisal appears to be an integral part of the school's staff development plan, aimed at enhancing children's learning through improving the skills of all professional staff members, and developing an effective support team through developing the skills of all staff members (p. 99). The approach adopted involves teacher self appraisal, a "consultative" or "buddy" component where teachers work in pairs to look at each other's work, and appraisal by senior staff. For example, one head teacher stated (p. 22):

> I visit classrooms on a regular basis. There are three occasions during the year when the classrooms are visited formally. As well, there are the informal times and there is also the time when the teacher is involved in their own appraisal. On the basis of this I ask the teacher to evaluate the areas that they believe are the most important for further staff development and this is taken into account when I draw up the budget.

Teacher appraisal may also use information gathered from the school community. In several schools this was quite formalised through surveys of parents, in others the Chair of the School Board conducted a series of randomly selected but structured interviews with whomever he/she wished.

The report from the New Zealand teacher seminars (New Zealand Ministry of Education, 1993) provides teachers' perspectives on the appraisal system. In response to the question "How would you like to be judged as a teacher?" and "How are you judged?", the participants indicated general agreement with the processes outlined. As stated in the report (p. 42):

> The group were prepared to be held accountable for the things over which they had control, but not over those matters outside their bailiwick. Social, environmental and economic issues came into this category. Any evaluation should be in terms of agreed upon objectives that had been negotiated but were also open for renegotiation if conditions changed.

The logical link with staff development was suggested by the teachers, as they asked (*ibid.*):

> What is the point of admitting needs unless there are the resources and the opportunities to meet those needs and to satisfy them? Any evaluation of this kind needs to be regular and ongoing with discussion and debate, as apposed to a one-off discrete exercise.

It is interesting to note that there is uneven attention to teacher appraisal in the country reports. Some countries have well-developed policies which have been implemented and appear to be working. Other countries have chosen not to devote resources to this at the moment, perhaps on the basis that their educational systems are relatively centralised and it is felt the extra managerial lever is not needed. In the countries where appraisal was evident, the policy documents emphasised that it was part of the larger issue of staff development.

Increased responsibility for individual schools

As stated in Chapter 1, a policy area where there has been a similar development in many countries is the devolution of increased responsibility to individual schools.

The country reports describe how policies to give schools more responsibility for their own development have emerged from the evolution of educational reform. In the United States, for example, White and Roesch (1993) describe it in the following way (p. 33):

> Over the past fifty years as the US has faced different issues besetting their schools and society, educational reforms and changes were proposed that addressed curriculum, special populations of students, teacher preparation, and school re-organisation.
>
> In the 1950s, the national shock at Sputnik generated widespread support for curriculum reform movements in math, science and social science education. During the civil rights era Congress targeted special populations of students for remediation. It funded Head Start (1964) and the Elementary and Secondary Act of 1965 to provide additional resources, for example, in Title I and Title VII, for poor, minority, and non-English speaking students to perform better in schools.
>
> Teaching was to be professionalized, for example by creating a career ladder (Carnegie Forum, 1986; Holmes Group, 1986). Calls for giving teachers more pay, respect, and independence and autonomy in educational decision making were linked with increased accountability, often in the form of mandating minimal competency testing for teachers.
>
> Other reforms focused on changing policies and management at the local level of the school. The effective schools movement began by studying urban schools where test scores were above averages expected for poor and minority children. Advocates argued that schools could be improved if they have strong principals, who acted as instructional leaders, established a clear sense of mission, insisted on safety and order, and set specific achievement test score goals for students.

The policies referred to by White and Roesch are characterised not by small, incremental steps which continually modify and improve policy but by major philosophical and political shifts. The range of policy initiatives and foci of attention have been comprehensive, relating as they do to students, teachers, curriculum and school organisation and management. The breadth of action has reflected, at various times, the particular concerns of the community as expressed by their legislators, the deliberations of "blue-ribbon" committees, which have responded to particular needs, and to some extent to educational researchers and administrators.

The New Zealand case study (Ramsay, 1993) gives a detailed account of how the policy to devolve responsibility to individual schools came about. It began with expert committees to review and recommend a change in early childhood, primary and tertiary education. Ramsay (p. 2) locates the initial press for the policy examination within one arm of the government bureaucracy. He writes that the Department of Treasury, who were responsible for economic advice, wrote a brief for the re-elected Labour Government in 1987, which argued that "education was not fostering equity, participation, or achievement; that it was marked by 'middle-class capture'; and that the 'inputs' were not producing the 'outputs' (*i.e.* the Government was not receiving value for money)". The brief further argued that the State's role in education should move away from "provision" and focus more on providing parents with information so that they could make more informed choices about where they sent their children to school.

The New Zealand Government established a task force in 1987 to consider issues of delegation, flexibility and responsiveness in primary schools. The task force subsequently reported that the existing administrative system was cumbersome and inflexible, overcentralised, and had unnecessary overlaps between the central office, regional offices and education boards. In 1989 the government legislated to decentralise responsibility for the administration individual schools (Ramsay, 1993, p. 4):

> In summary, the movement towards devolution and local school management in both financial, decision making, and curriculum development represents an interesting balance between local control and central government. For example, local schools were expected, through a charter to define their own goals – but within a tightly constrained and particularised framework.

This observation suggests how a policy can be both facilitating and constraining as central governments strive to balance competing priorities in the face of many diverse and intangible factors. This means that not all consequences can be anticipated in "national" consideration of controversial public issues. Ramsay comments (p. 12):

> Tracking national policy to classroom practices (...) is very difficult indeed, and the problem has been under scrutiny for a number of years.

In light of these factors therefore, one important implication for the recent reforms of New Zealand's education administration emerges. It concerns the frame assumed by the policy. The reforms focused on shifting power and decision making from the central administration to local schools which the reformers believed would ultimately improve effective practice. The literature however, shows that removing constraints between central and local control does not in itself ensure more effective practice.

In developing its own programmes, the individual school may benefit from an external "audit". As indicated by the New Zealand Ministry of Education (1993, p. 28): "The review of a total school's performance in terms of its objectives can validate and communicate to the community at large the excellence or otherwise of the education being delivered by the particular school under review."

On the other hand, in the New Zealand teacher seminars which were conducted as part of the project, there was general agreement that the move to local self-management of schools had had a significant positive impact on schools. As reported (p. 49):

The absence of an inspectorate also gave teachers greater scope for innovation and creativity rather than needing to comply with the accepted and official wisdom. As such, local self-management facilitated quality teaching.

European countries are also using school plans and school-based curriculum development. In Sweden, for example, Lander (1993, p. 114) reports:

> Since 1980 comprehensive schools have been compelled to do working plans. The implementation of them was very slow during the decade (Ekholm *et al.*, 1987), but it is likely that the political school plans will stimulate the use of working plans, especially since the inflow of resources will eventually be tied to good planning and evaluation results. Another stimulus for working plans is the recent decision by parliament to introduce a voucher-like allocation system for preschools and schools. The earlier quest to make local curricula profiles now has additional meaning, as schools will compete with another for pupils. The need to adjust to the "parental market" will in that case also influence developmental planning within schools.

As described in Chapter 3, Norway in 1987 enacted national curriculum guidelines that require each school to participate in specifying its own curriculum, and they were directed to carry out self-improvement projects. (Subsequently, a new wave of curriculum development has taken place in Norway.) Educational policy in Finland also has shown a pronounced shift toward more autonomy for schools in curriculum and instructional methods.

In Austria, the case-study report (Altrichter *et al.*, 1993) sees a growing trend for reform which is fostered by teachers. There are signs that initiatives to allow schools more autonomy will be implemented. Such changes would reduce the traditional influence of what is termed "legalism and bureaucratisation", which help to maintain the rights of clients but also tend to stifle initiative. A consequence of the traditional approach is that teachers and schools previously have been "deprived of all creativity and ingenuity which seem to be preconditions of quality education" (p. 4).

Conclusion

The country studies were not designed to yield a complete catalogue of policies affecting teachers. On the contrary, most of them were highly selective in focusing on a single policy or a small set of them. Nevertheless, even this very incomplete listing suggests the multiplicity of policies that impinge on schools and teachers. There is a real danger of policies piling up and paralysing schools and teachers. How can policy makers keep innovation alive without sinking those who have to implement the policies? As reported by teachers in the US country report (White and Roesch, 1993, p. 94):

> Several suggested that every time a new requirement is added, policy makers should identify a policy or regulation that can be dropped. One teacher explained that, "a lot has been put on their plates", and they would like to slow down for several years and get current initiatives working right before we are given more to do.

The next chapter will consider how effective schools are able to make use of central policies without being overwhelmed by them.

Chapter 6

Quality Schools

This chapter describes a set of school-level conditions or factors that influence the quality of teaching and the implementation of policy to improve it. In undertaking this analysis it is important to repeat that the case studies do not represent prevailing practice in their own countries. Nevertheless, the consistency of findings across the case studies from different countries, and the consonance of the case studies and teacher seminars with the literature on school effectiveness and school improvement, do suggest that the conclusions drawn in this chapter have some generalisability.

As we have seen in previous chapters, the interrelationships between concepts of teacher quality, policies designed to enhance them, and the context of schooling is highly complex. Yet two broad generalisations stand out from the national cases that are worth considering at this early stage.

The first is that teacher quality defined in terms of the individuality, intelligence, artistry, grace and fluidity of individual teachers has a powerful influence on student learning. This conclusion radiates across the cultural boundaries of the case studies. This individual artistry, however, is nurtured by a strong schoolwide emphasis on teamwork, collaboration and risk-taking. The conditions supportive of such an approach to teaching are characteristic of specific school contexts. Not all schools, for many different reasons, are supportive of the work of teachers in this way.

The second general conclusion to be drawn from the cases is the difficulty policy initiatives have in penetrating the context of schooling. The implementation of national policy and its relationship to classroom practice is, as is well known from other work, notoriously fickle. Yet the school-level context can facilitate, and to a great extent determine, successful policy implementation. The Austrian case, for example, provides some evidence that the more coherent and collaborative the internal conditions of the school, the more knowledge teachers in those schools have of national policy initiatives. In these and many other instances where staff commitment has been very high, the outcomes secured were unusually impressive.

These two conclusions must be viewed against the "macro" policy context. In most OECD countries there appear to be seemingly contradictory pressures for centralisation on the one hand (*i.e.* increasing government control over policy and direction), and decentralisation on the other (*i.e.* more responsibility for implementation, resource management and evaluation at the local level). This tension is making it very difficult for schools and local authorities to implement successfully innovations that make a real difference to the quality of schooling and pupil achievement. The key challenge, as a recent OECD report makes clear, is to find a balance between the increasing demands for centrally determined policy initiatives and quality control, and the encouragement of locally developed school improvement efforts (OECD, 1989a, p. 2).

A general response to the dilemma of decentralisation has been to give more responsibility to schools for their own management. Although this goes by different names in different countries – "local management of schools" in Britain; "self-managing schools" in Australia; "site-based management" or "restructuring" in the United States – the concept remains similar. Unfortunately, similarity does not imply clarity or specificity. Many of the policies seem to be either politically or ideologically inspired, or an *ad hoc* response to an immediate "crisis" situation. Simply changing bureaucratic procedures or holding people more accountable does not by itself improve the quality of education for our young people.

The case studies suggest that those schools that are surviving with flair during this era of change exhibit a predisposition towards school improvement that equips them to take maximum advantage of external circumstances. However strong the forces for reform, a commitment to internal development may offer the best way of dealing with such pressure. There appears to be a consonance between internal priority and external opportunity. Unless schools are able to take a more proactive stance towards external policy initiatives and translate them into needs at the school level, they will suffer from innovation overload and gradually lose control of their own educational agenda. To put it another way, it is the "culture of the school" that sustains the improvement process and ensures enhanced outcomes for students. This is why the local context is so important in any discussion of teacher quality.

Characteristics of quality schools

Research on effective schools concluded that schools do make a difference in student achievement and other outcomes. There was also agreement that differences in outcome are systematically related to variations in the school's climate, culture or ethos. Furthermore, the culture of the school is amenable to alteration by concerted action on the part of the school staff. Although this is not an easy task, the evidence suggested that teachers and schools had more control than they may have imagined over their ability to change their present situation. More recent research also has reaffirmed the influence of schools, and even departments within schools, on teachers' professionalism (Talbert and McLaughlin, 1994).

What then makes this concerted action possible? The analysis of the case studies suggests that there are eight characteristics of those schools that display a high level of teacher quality. In brief, they are:

Vision and values

A strong values base is perhaps a necessary condition in schools that have high levels of teacher quality.

Organisation of teaching and learning

Schools supportive of teacher quality have developed ways to organise teaching and learning in support of student achievement. Deliberate and self-conscious experimentation and adaptation of the organisation of teaching and learning is a characteristic feature of those schools with a predominance of "quality" teachers.

Management arrangements

Schools celebrating high levels of teacher quality have modified their internal organisation to support such an aspiration. This is particularly true of the existence of teams and collaborative working arrangements in such schools. The "management arrangements" in such schools also include structures for managing time and resources, staffing and recruitment.

Policy formation process

This refers to the school's process for identifying priorities, planning, implementation and evaluation. This is often an evolutionary, experiential rather than bureaucratic process.

Leadership

Refers both to the role of the "senior management team" in a school as well as to the encouragement of leadership for specific developments from those at all levels in the school. The nurturing and dispersal of leadership throughout the school necessitates a dramatic change in traditional concepts of the head or principal, and requires specific training.

Staff development

Many schools develop "infrastructures" to support the professional development of staff. There are links here with specific policies for teacher quality such as teacher appraisal as well as connections to other aspects of management arrangements such as planning and resource allocation.

Relationships with community and district

Many successful schools establish powerful links with and are responsive to their communities from which they generate some of their core values. Relationships with external agencies also appear important for sustaining teacher quality.

Culture of the school

The culture, spirit and ethos of the school is notoriously difficult to pin down. One major element of school cultures that exhibit high levels of teacher quality, however, is the encouragement of risk-taking and experimentation.

In the following sections of this chapter each of these characteristics is described in more detail by reference to examples taken from the case studies. Inevitably, there is a high degree of overlap among the characteristics. They build on and feed from each other, and this is how it should be. The analytic device of identifying and describing individual characteristics, although helpful at an expository level, distorts reality. So there are many links made, both explicit and implicit, between the various sections of this chapter. The use of case-study extracts as examples of the various characteristics is purely illustrative. There is no implication that just because a case is quoted it is either exemplary or representative of any particular national context. The extracts have been chosen because of their appositeness to a particular point. The other but subordinate selection criterion has been to ensure an adequate representation from the national cases and the schools they described.

Vision and values

It is very clear from the case studies that schools exhibiting high levels of teacher quality and student achievement are characterised by a vision and a strong and shared values base. Vision and values are much abused and fuzzy concepts. It is not so much what the vision and values are, but rather that the school recognises their importance. Many of the case-study schools have a "vision" that is directly related to the development of students, which in turn has clear implications for teaching and teacher collaboration. This general thought is well captured in the conclusions to the Australian case studies (McRae, 1993, pp. 112-113):

> An "uncluttered" vision relentlessly focused on student needs and success was evident generally, but in three of the schools it was remarkably and unusually obvious. "Uncluttered" was a term used by the principal of one of these schools and exactly catches the flavour of this direct and dominant influence. Nothing was to stand in its way. It had a profound influence on staff behaviour and was a clear binding force. In simple form the common sentiment appeared to be "students come first" meaning not just some but *all* students (...). There was also an unusually high degree of support. Teachers' attitudes and needs were consistently considered, professional development and the state of teachers' morale were central

concerns (...). Initiatives in five of the schools and arguably the sixth were dominated by forms of teacher collaboration. Evidence collected through these case studies suggests that of all forms of collaboration, collaborative planning of teaching has the most impact on teacher satisfaction and teaching quality.

The sustaining power of such visions was a continuing theme in many schools, as seen in the following comment from the United States case study (White and Roesch, 1993, p. 59):

> I notice a hand-written yellowing sheet of newsprint up on the door of the conference room. When I comment on the chart Mr Oden says that he used it in an in-service with his faculty when he first came to Heron five years ago. "It's everything I believe in. I've kept it up ever since."

The chart read:

> "Good Instructional Practices
> – Variety of learning experiences
> – Reasons for activities
> – Frequent checks for understanding
> – Risk taking."

This sustaining power of a vision, however, is not restricted to the school, it can also pervade a whole school district or educational authority. Witness the conclusions drawn by the US case-study writer (p. 84):

> The quality of teaching is strongly related to the extent that teachers believe that all students can succeed. A corollary belief includes the commitment to educating the whole child: to meeting the social, emotional, academic, and physical needs of the students. These teachers also believe that it is important to be up-to-date in knowledge and pedagogy for their subject area; to find ways to link academic knowledge with what students already know and with what students want to learn; and to have a vision of how knowledge taught in schools will be useful for students in the world outside of school.

> These teachers talked about and treated even their most troubling and troublesome students with empathy, respect, and dignity. Teachers observed in these seven schools passionately sought (and frequently developed) innovative and meaningful activities and programmes that would enable their students to succeed.

The important point is not the vision in abstract or as an artefact, but the motivation and guidance it gives to teachers in their daily work. Seen in this way, the vision of a school is strongly linked to, and influences the whole, context of the school. "Vision" can have a profound impact on teacher motivation and behaviour, as is evident in this quotation from the Austrian case study (Altrichter et al., 1993, p. 40):

> I've done my job with varying intensity. In schools with a bad climate I've naturally tried to be off as soon as possible. Here work is important for everybody. I've been in schools where everybody was making the working hours pass and then was leaving the school in greatest possible haste. And the head was the first one to leave – you could see the biggest clouds of dust behind him. This school is more than a

place of doing classroom work. Sometimes you stay a little longer and work on something which also could be done at home. You do this at school because here is a good atmosphere – and therefore you are ready to do a little more.

Obviously vision does not just happen. It develops in a dynamic way, often as a result of conflict and negotiation. The process of establishing a vision is complex but necessary if high levels of teacher quality are to be achieved and sustained. Consider the following two examples taken from the Austrian and Australian cases (McRae, 1993, pp. 31-32):

School A (an academic upper-secondary school in Austria) is particularly interesting in this respect because its cultural cohesion did not come easy (and still is a dynamic matter of conflict and negotiation): Traditionalist views of schooling are in competition with more modern ones, an orientation towards "high student achievement" and towards a "student-friendly atmosphere", a traditional strength in science and complementary learning with respect to humanities and social responsibility have their representatives in the school. The school's idea is to balance and integrate different educational philosophies, qualifications, and personalities of different departments into some more comprehensive philosophy of the school. What are the mechanisms for doing that?

– There is a *"mission statement"* formulating some image of the school as integrating different strengths.
– This statement has been discussed and approved by a staff meeting.
– The head is *frequently, publicly and plausibly* referring to the mission statement, trying to locate the place diverse initiatives occupy in the geography of this statement.
– The head is *supported* in his integrative endeavours by representatives of the parents' and of the personnel associations.
– The whole *communicative climate* of the school is considered open and fruitful by most interviewees and seems to reward activity, engagement, and achievement of staff.

At the beginning of 1991 the leadership team (of Hincks Avenue Primary School in Australia) met for a week before school began, to sort out their values and beliefs to make sure they were on the same path. "We felt it was essential to operate as a team with a set of consistent values", the current principal said, "otherwise nothing would work. You must have common values when the going gets tough." The staff were then involved in developing a statement of values that were intended to be reflective of their practice. These focused on trust, open communication, team work, individual dignity and worth.

"We also felt that it was important to state them publicly and make them a feature of the school." This is what we believe in. These are our priorities. "You could make sense of things for people." This preoccupation with being very direct and concrete about what is to happen, how and what the outcomes should be like for all those involved with the school, is one of its striking features.

It took several months of trialing and review to get the values and decision-making procedures in place and working practically.

"Our two overriding concerns at that stage – the acting principal again – were the professional growth of teachers and the development of commitment to achieving the whole-school goals." The focal point for both of these issues was the development of a role statement for teachers. This grew from two sources – ideas from a departmental document and collaborative development by the staff. This role statement is quite obviously a powerful document taken very seriously and "lived out", rather than just another piece of paper in the office filing cabinet.

"It's vital to have personnel who are learners, committed and work as a team. Collaboration and making sure there is consistency right across the school are the keys." As might be anticipated, these changes were not appreciated by all members of staff initially, but within a short time all staff began to see the benefits which were accruing and became enthusiastic in their support.

As these examples suggest, vision and an agreement on shared values appears to be characteristic of schools that have high levels of teacher quality. Vision is usually related to a sense of "moral purpose" – having a positive impact on students. This has obvious and direct implications for teaching and teacher development. Visions that serve this purpose are not given – by the principal or government – but evolve over time through conflict and negotiation. By the same token, visions are also not exclusive. There may be multiple-value bases existing in large schools but, when successful, they are complementary rather than contradictory. Vision in this ideal sense does not deny the personal values of individual teachers, rather it provides a guiding framework for the school as a whole. Over time, however, their permissiveness can become extremely powerful and, as is seen later, conditions the whole context of schooling.

Organisation of teaching and learning

One of the most powerful direct influences of the visions and values of a school is on the organisation of teaching and learning. In this admittedly selective sample of case-study schools that have high levels of teacher quality, there are very clear links between vision and values on the one hand and the organisation of teaching and learning on the other. The vision in these schools reflects a strong commitment to the progress and development of young people, and this has practical implications not just for teaching learning and assessment within the school but also for the ways in which teachers work together.

There are four aspects of the organisation of teaching and learning in particular that are raised in the case studies: *a)* organisation of teaching and learning driven by values rather than by bureaucratic expediency; *b)* the organisation of teaching and learning at the classroom level, especially the physical organisation of students; *c)* the organisation of teachers' work to permit collaboration; *d)* and the forms of assessment and curriculum development.

The link between vision and the organisation of teaching and learning is clearly seen in the description of Moisio School in the Finnish Case Study (Hämäläinen and Jokela, 1993, pp. 47-48):

> Since its foundation in the mid-1950s the Moisio School has enjoyed an excellent reputation. With great changes occurring in the world around it there was a concern in the school to examine the way in which it operated. Changes began to take place in the middle of the 1980s. The main goal, to adopt a more holistic approach to learning, was agreed upon unanimously. However, it was unclear how to attain this goal. A starting point was a systematic search for information. The teachers became acquainted with different views and approaches in the field of education. In addition to Freinet pedagogy, the school has also been influenced by the humanistic psychology of education. The starting point of both approaches has been primarily to value and respect the human being (the child).
>
> The original routines of the school began to change so dramatically that the school began to describe itself as offering an open-learning environment. In an open-learning environment the main emphasis of school work shifts from the teacher to the pupil and from teaching to learning. Instead of learning isolated fragments of information, stress was laid on skills in acquiring and processing information. Another important goal was to foster pupils' individuality. In spite of the fact that the basis of the school's operation was the curriculum provided by the municipality, the goal was to adapt it flexibly in accordance with the interests of individuals.
>
> The object of changes was to place the pupil at the centre of the school's activities. The teachers believe in the positive growth of the child. A pupil plans and evaluates his own work. He plays a greater role in selecting learning objectives, contents and means. It is hoped that invention and understanding will come from the child, although the initial input may come from the teacher.
>
> The teacher is the person who introduces new learning and makes the initial move. The teacher tutors and assists in tackling tasks. Planning and organising work is part of the teacher's role rather than simply imparting knowledge. Work in the classrooms is only occasionally led by the teacher because many tasks and projects are undertaken using a pupil-centred approach. At the same time pupils learn to take responsibility for their own work.

The modification of the ways in which teaching and learning are organised in order to meet the schools' dominant values is found in most case studies. In the Australian case (McRae, p. 7):

> Perhaps the most significant changes noted were those designed to promote greater student participation in and responsibility for learning. In several schools it was easy to see the links between organisational change and changes to pedagogy and student approaches to learning, both intended and unintended. One more common example observed was the consolidation of the curriculum in the early secondary years to reduce curriculum fragmentation and to enable timetabling of more flexible, often longer, teaching/learning sessions. In some schools, however, quite young primary students are evidently benefiting from and enjoying having a range of specialist teachers. The National Schools Project has, at this early stage, demonstrated poten-

tial as a useful laboratory for examining the range of costs and benefits of various forms of organisation.

The organisation of teaching and learning at the classroom level also implies changes to the classroom environment in line with the vision and values of the teacher and the school, and the principles underlying teaching and learning. The primary schools in the Swedish case (Lander, 1993, pp. 13-14) provide a graphic example:

How to place the pupils physically in the classroom of primary schools is normally up to the individual teacher's decision. For all but one of the "non-graded classrooms", collective decisions have been taken in order to get large tables at which groups of five to ten children can work together or individually, but easily co-operate. Children still have individual places at the tables.

Out of eleven "graded classrooms" only one uses the classical equipment with single benches in rows all pointing in one direction. In four rooms, benches are placed in pairs, all in one direction. In six classrooms, pupils sit four to six together in groups, benches placed between each other with no special direction but so that everybody can see the blackboard.

There is thus no doubt that primary teachers in our sample prefer working-places that permit co-operation. At the same time, the large tables give more space free in the room, allowing more wandering about which is essential for the working pattern often used. They also give large spaces for materially big jobs. One teacher puts forward the positive functions of large tables when she helps individual pupils: this at the same time permits her to have some control of what the other children at the same table are doing, both in terms of work-efforts and in terms of learning.

None of the observed classrooms in primary schools had the teacher's desk placed in the classical front position before the pupils' benches. It was usually placed in the corner not far from the blackboard and often occupied by working-materials. The placement of the teacher's own table underlines symbolically that her management functions does not need a "royal" status in the focus of everybody's attention and from where she herself with an eagle's eye can supervise everybody at the same time. In fact, all teachers observed were constantly walking around or sitting close to pupils except for the rather few moments when they did blackboard work.

There was also evidence that changes in teaching were reflected in the ways teachers collaborated and worked together. Collaboration was a continuing theme as seen in these examples from the Australian (McRae, p. 7), Finland (Hämäläinen and Jokela, p. 43) and the United States (White and Roesch, p. 22) case studies:

Australia – There is evidence that the NSP [National Schools Project] has encouraged a sense of control and ownership by teachers of their own work. Teachers have gained the time to reflect on their teaching practice and that of their colleagues. Teachers have gained opportunities to work more collaboratively. There were many examples of successful professional collaboration and its benefits: reduced isolation and gains in flexibility; shared responsibility leading to reduction in levels of stress; greater consistency of approach; and the value of and challenge and stimulation resulting from pooled expertise. There is also evidence that collaboration takes time, patience and involves some additional stress.

Finland – The teachers appeared to benefit considerably from this method of group work where each can contribute their own ideas. It would be difficult for a teacher acting alone to generate such a large variety of ideas or resources. With such common planning teachers can benefit from one another's strengths. For example, one teacher may have fresh ideas, another may have insights offered by experience, another may have the ability to increase the pace of work and another may have artistic skills. One of the teachers stated that: "more than half of the pleasure I get from my work comes from collaboration." According to the teachers the collaboration not only helps in the concrete planning of work but has psychological benefits. During these meetings teachers can discuss their problems and anxieties as well as their successes. The teachers explained that they related their experiences in an open manner rather than implying or hinting at issues. This is of considerable importance in maintaining their mental well-being and in controlling stress. Teachers well-being also affects pupils. One teacher who was interviewed observed: "When the teacher feels happy, the pupils also feel happy."

United States – Their collaborative teams provide such satisfaction, support and inspiration (as reported in Chapter 5 and in this teacher's comment: "As my comfort level in classroom teaching grows, more risk-taking occurs. I am getting support from both teachers and the administration.")

The organisation of teaching and learning and teacher collaboration also affects forms of assessment and curriculum development within the school. An example of assessment is provided by the Italian case (Macconi, 1993, pp. 43-44):

There are significantly common issues that provide a profile of "in search schools": that is, schools who are looking for improvement in knowledge, professional skills, community involvement, open possibilities for innovation and quality improvement.

Individually each school has its own approach to assessment. Franchi (for example) has an outstanding School Prospectus in which cultural decisions and activities have a theoretical justification... They state that the choice of general objectives explains the style of the school while the interdisciplinary approach typifies the school culture and remedial support and development work.

Some schools are very detailed in the description of necessary performances, some define assessment as progressive approach to expected outcomes, some propose study seminars. It seems as if everybody is concerned about assessment and control of processes, wide issues and specific ones such as workshops and labs. They all agree on the need to study outcomes data before planning again and to reflect on possible implications.

There are also curriculum implications to the organisation of teaching and learning as is also seen in the Italian case (p. 45):

The pedagogic culture is made explicit through various kinds of planning. Indicators of these choices are:
– cross-curricular objectives;
– contents and necessary competencies to acquire them;
– mental operations stimulated by various subjects;

- consistency between general and specific objectives;
- methods implemented in order to facilitate learning.

They talk in terms of "conceptual network", of confrontation between personal knowledge and conventional knowledge, of use of different methodologies and strategies in order to build quality. They reflect on subject epistemology in order to allow all students to approach different levels of knowledge.

The point that is being illustrated in this section is that schools with high levels of teacher quality tend to make clear decisions about the organisation of teaching and learning. In many schools this organisation assumes a "taken for granted" aspect, which is not to underestimate its impact on the daily life of teachers and students. Illustrations of the chosen teaching forms are found in Chapter 4 and are not therefore treated in any detail here. What is important in regard to the context of schooling, however, is the sustaining power of collaboration among teachers, which is a consistent feature of the case studies.

It is the collaboration fed by a vision that appears to sustain the changes in teaching and learning. Modifications in a school's bureaucratic arrangements are by themselves insufficient. Fully as important but less well documented is the role of assessment, curriculum development and co-ordination. Although these could all be regarded in some senses as aspects of the school's management arrangements described in the following section, the organisation of teaching and learning has been treated separately because of its close links to teacher quality and the "vision" of the school.

Management arrangements

The term "management arrangements" describes those aspects of the school's organisation which are chosen by the members of an organisation to help them to conduct their affairs and realise their aims. There is an endless possible variety of management arrangements. They vary according to the size, type and phase of the school as well as to the preferences of the governors, head and staff. Although there is not an ideal set of arrangements, there are three main dimensions common to all sets of management arrangements (Hargreaves and Hopkins, 1991, p. 16):

The first consists of frameworks which guide the actions of all who are involved in the school. Examples of frameworks are the school's aims and policies, and the systems for decision making and consultation. Without clear frameworks, the school would soon lapse into confusion and conflict.

Secondly, the management arrangements clarify roles and responsibilities. All who are involved in the school need to have a shared understanding of their respective roles and of who is taking responsibility for what. Well designed frameworks are useless without clear roles and responsibilities.

Thirdly, the management arrangements promote ways in which the people involved can work together so that each person finds their particular role enjoyable and rewarding, and at the same time the aims of the school as a whole can be achieved successfully.

To devise management arrangements that solve the problems inherent in these three dimensions is a challenging task. Yet this challenge is already being attended to in many case-study schools. A commitment to "teacher quality" requires every school to re-think the nature of management: what it is and what it needs to become. An example of this is provided by the contrast between Birch and Elm Secondary schools in the following extract from the Swedish case study (Lander, 1993, pp. 7-8). Although only focusing on a single aspect of the schools' management arrangements, it is interesting to see how far the schools' internal organisation has been adapted to reflect both external and internal change.

> There is a significant difference between the two schools in how they use study-leaders and working-units. Working-units (*i.e.* groupings of teachers who work together) were made obligatory by the national curriculum of 1980. This organisational form at the beginning was not popular at all among teachers, but during the second half of the eighties primary schools increasingly implemented it. The change among secondary schools was considerably slower. It is not unusual that schools say that they formally have one working-unit for the staff, *i.e.* have kept the traditional organisation with a common staff-meeting and subject departments. Up till 1992 Birch school followed this model. But then it decided to split up into two working-units. Elm school, on the other hand, was one of the earliest schools in the country to adopt the working-unit, and has organised the staff in three such units. Pupil care is the most important duty of the working-units.
>
> Elm school is somewhat larger than Birch school. Nevertheless it has only five study-leaders. They all have considerable time for their duties. All have between 6 and 12 hours a week. At Birch school there are thirteen study-leaders, twelve have 2 hours a week, or less, for this job. One has more. The Birch school model reflects the dominance of the subject department organisation, in which every subject ought to have one "head subject master" in charge of books and other utensils. The Elm school model is a radical departure from the traditional organisation. At both schools there are study-leaders with special responsibility for pupil care. At Elm school they also take responsibility for broader subject areas while they are specialised to certain subjects at Birch school.

The following extracts from the US case study (White and Roesch, pp. 86-93) illustrates many important facets to the modifications of a school's management arrangements.

- The change to a school-based planning and assessment process takes years to accomplish and requires skilled support from both the local school administration and specialists within the central administration such as the Office of Educational Planning Services.
- At the schools where collaborative decision making has been going on the longest, examples are emerging indicating that the nature of the problems being solved changes and becomes more comprehensive, in-depth, and participatory.
- There are overlapping change groups within the school, formal and informal networks, and an emphasis on multiple forms of communication.

- The schools characterised by collaborative decision making are flexible, quickly able to allow for innovation, but slow to commit to long-term changes.
- Many policies are successfully implemented because vertical lines of communication are maintained in this school system.
- Groups of teachers and administrators use school district programs as vehicles to effect organization change and improve instruction. However, different schools utilize different programs and policies in different ways as vehicles for change.
- Many of these changes developed through the collaborative decision making of teachers at the school level could not have occurred without the prior existence and support of system-wide policies and programs that developed and maintained a strong curriculum and a well-educated, high performance cadre of teachers.

These "headlines" taken from US case study do little more than signal the important issues which we lack space to discuss fully. The fundamental point, however, should be clear. It is that schools that exhibit high levels of teacher quality have over time modified their internal conditions to explicitly support quality in teaching. This is more than having a vision or altering the learning arrangements in a few classrooms. These schools have systematically, although no doubt at times intuitively, sought to bring their total organisation in line with their philosophical commitment to student progress and quality learning. This is no "quick-fix" approach to school improvement, more a radical re-orientation of organisational purpose. Without it, however, quality teaching and student achievement will not be sustained. It is this commitment to restructuring that characterises those schools who have succeeded in solving the centralisation-decentralisation conundrum. Although this remains a background factor in many case studies, it is fundamentally characteristic of all schools that display the same grace and fluidity as do their teachers and students. Most of the individual aspects of the "context of schooling" described in this chapter stem from this key idea.

An additional point needs to be added here. An important strategy used to maintain high levels of teacher quality in many case-study schools was the recruitment of staff. Appointing teachers who share a similar philosophy is an obvious yet important way of sustaining high levels of teacher quality.

Policy formation process

The policy formation process, like the organisation of teaching and learning, is a specific aspect of the school's management arrangements. As with the organisation of teaching and learning it requires separate discussion because of its particular relevance to teacher quality. In the same way as the organisation of teaching and learning reflects the practical application of a school's commitment to teaching and teacher development, so does the policy formation process signal a school's ability to adapt to changing circumstance within the context of its own values base. This refers to the school's process for identifying priorities, planning, implementation and evaluation. This is often an evolutionary rather than a bureaucratic process.

One of the striking features of the case-study schools is that very few, if any, reacted in a positive or direct way to national or local policies. These comments by the Austrian case-study writers (Altrichter *et al.*, p. 33) are typical of many other schools and national cases:

> Teachers feel insufficiently informed towards national and regional initiatives. They feel that they have little say and influence on the concrete shape of national policies, they see national policies as (...) interference in the workings of the school.

> On the whole, it is surprising how few conducive influences from the national and regional level are perceived in particular by teachers.

> *a)* Interviewees are usually *not aware of specific national* policies pointed towards teacher quality nor of favourable frame conditions. Important national initiatives are not perceived at all or are not perceived to have had any influence on the quality of teaching and the school.

> *b)* If a range of comparatively positive "frame factors" may have contributed to the maintenance of quality in the school system (*e.g.* good standard of initial teacher training, comparatively good pay and good work conditions) these are not (any more) consciously perceived as such by our interviewees.

A possible interpretation could be that national initiatives have been *too diffuse* (too little concerted) and *too little publicised* to have entered the awareness of the people at the base of the system.

The Austrian case-study writers (p. 34) then go on to describe different ways in which schools react to challenges: "The ways schools perceive, look for, develop, and make use of room for manœuvre for their internal and external development represent in our view telling characteristics of organisational life and important preconditions for the development of schools as quality environments." When confronted with a challenge some schools primarily see a task which they are confident to cope with. They feel that they have influence and that they are able to shape their provisions and their organisational life themselves. On the other hand, there are schools who see – sometimes identical – challenges as burdens inflicted on them by external pressure which they are subjected to and have no power of escaping, modifying, or transforming. "Politically active schools" take initiative to analyse their situation and to develop some "philosophy" which represents shared educational values. They try to give these values some concrete form in their teaching and the social life of the school. They take care to organise their internal communication flow in a transparent and satisfying manner (which includes pupils) and to develop some steady exchange with their social environment. If they need external support they actively search for it.

It is this ideal type description that characterises those schools in the case studies that sustain high levels of teacher quality and are able to respond effectively to external demands while sustaining their own vision of their educational futures.

This "ideal school type" stands in contrast to the images created by the typical external policy context. The traditional national policy approach is well captured by this description of the Finnish experience with the rationalist approach of the 1970s (Hämäläinen and Jokela, pp. 4-5):

The rationalist approach has proved ineffective in Finnish comprehensive schools, because the teachers' local context, attitudes and opinions towards teaching, and interpretations of hierarchical changes have invalidated the results of extensive curriculum and study material projects. Detailed stage by stage development models – which sound highly technical in their use of verbs such as "build", "construct" and "design" – make teachers feel that curriculum planning is too complicated and that it had better be left to "experts". Instead, teachers use concrete study materials in their planning.

Many countries experience similar policy contexts. Increasingly, however, implementation strategies such as a school development plans are being suggested or mandated. Take for example the Norwegian situation (Baasland, 1993, pp. 34-35):

As part of the school development work, the schools should produce a school plan and annual report for the last four years. Contents and structure varies in these plans on the three schools; in principle, this is two types of plans contained in one:

"Activity plan": this may be regarded as an overall plan, partly to describe how the overall management of the school is seen in relation to existing frameworks for resources, main objectives and measures to achieve them; partly to indicate areas where the school can and should develop further.

This last part may be called:

"School development plan": stating the school's vision and development objectives, educational platform, a concrete plan for special priority areas/matters (distribution of responsibility and plan for progress), and a plan surveying required development of expertise and further education.

The school shall give a qualitative assessment of its own work in a minimum of one area. That is to say: the schools shall not only report back on whether any measures have been carried out, but also assess itself in accordance with a written plan including pre-formulated objectives. To conclude this, one can say that the work brought more "stress" than expected, one reason being that the assessment criteria had not been discussed in full, the formulation of objectives was vague, the participants were in need of more training and the schools were in different stages of opening up the classrooms for a full view.

A similar illustration is found in the English case (Baker *et al.*, 1993, pp. 12-13):

There was no common needs identification system operating across all four schools. Nonetheless each school was able to identify a range of institutional and personal training needs through a combination of formal and mostly, informal mechanisms. Such mechanisms were familiar to staff but were not always set out in, for example, a staff handbook.

Each school had a school development plan (SDP) which provided a framework for identifying training needs both for individuals and groups of staff. While most staff know of these documents, some were unaware of their significance and unfamiliar with their content. The degree of familiarity varied from school to school.

The analysis of a school's current position in terms of strengths, weaknesses, opportunities and threats (SWOT) proved to be useful in the formulation and review of SDPs.

Appraisal systems also contributed to needs identification. Where they were in place they provided a means of preparing individual action plans, linked to plans for institutional development. In the best practice, this individual action planning, with reference to a detailed job description, made precise references to training – training intended to meet the declared objectives of the individual and directly or indirectly the quality of teaching and learning in the department and/or the school. The effectiveness of such individual action plans was reviewed annually by the teacher and head teacher. However, many part-time and supply teachers were not yet being appraised.

Appraisal systems were not fully integrated with SDPs. The former tended to focus on the professional needs of individual staff which did not necessarily marry with the development needs of the school as a whole.

Implementation strategies for national policies such as a school development plan, teacher appraisal systems and school self-evaluation are, as these examples illustrate, difficult themselves to implement. They are, however, worth persevering with as they serve the twin purpose noted earlier of providing a mechanism for implementing policy at the same time as strengthening the school's capacity for managing internal as well as external change.

An interesting description of how teachers manage this process is given by one of the US case-study schools (White and Roesch, pp. 51-52):

Eagle teachers carefully consider each new policy that is introduced for change. Although on the cutting edge of many changes in the County themselves, they are willing to voice objections to top-down policies that they do not think are carefully thought through.

The following narrative describes how two teachers carefully researched and implemented the policy of including learning disabled students [LD] in a regular classroom:

We saw a need to team students and general education students in a combined class. We felt it would help LD Students develop more appropriate social skills and improve their social acceptance in the school. This was also influenced by the fact that we were going to need to share rooms due to the expansion of the school day from 6 to 7 periods. This change required full-year science classes instead of semester classes. A new general-education teacher was hired and small LD classes lost teaching space. This gave us a chance to suggest this to the principal. We developed a plan to implement this teaming program. We decided to document our experience with this teamed class through teacher research.

Numerous policies impacted this teaming effort. We asked that the number of students in the class be limited and that only 25 per cent of them be LD students. We asked that the class be heterogeneous regarding ability and gender. We requested common planning time. We gradually (over a three-year period) received this requested support. In addition, the county and administration supported our teacher research with substitute coverage on days we participated in our teacher research activities.

Schools able to marry the often conflicting and competing demands for both external and internal change display unusually high levels of organisational sophistication. It is this aspect of their management arrangements that enables them to sustain high levels of teacher quality over the long term.

Leadership

In this section it is important to distinguish between effective administration as traditionally conceived and a broadened structure of leadership (with its corresponding policy implications). In other words, the role of the "senior management team" in a school as well as the encouragement of leadership for specific developments from those at all levels in the school. The idea is well summarised in the Australian case-study report (McRae, p. 7):

> It was not surprising that some of the schools that had progressed most in rethinking the links between the organisation of teaching and learning outcomes for students were schools with strong leadership teams and where the leadership team had a strong identification with the school and its community.

The nurturing and dispersal of leadership throughout the school necessitates a dramatic change in traditional concepts of the head or principal and requires specific training. This is another conundrum that schools which are able to sustain high levels of teacher quality are able to resolve. The New Zealand case (Ramsay, p. 64) gives a very clear indication of this ideal type role for the school principal:

> Almost without exception, the schools in our studies had principals who demonstrated a capacity for educational leadership. With the co-operation of their staffs and the Board of Trustees (BOT) they had developed a very clear-cut philosophical base for their schools. The charters were in place and contained some interesting innovative measures. In particular, the schools (...) had developed – under the leadership of the principal and senior staff – innovative measures of appraisal and professional staff development. The principals had also secured the confidence of not only their board, but the community at large... In summary, the principal of each of the schools had close relationships with staff members and the Board of Trustees, and had developed a clearly articulated philosophy in consultation with the community at large. The philosophy permeated the whole school and was subject to frequent and regular review.

> It is also interesting to note that in response to a question about the qualities they would look for in appointing a new principal the five chairpersons of the Boards of Trustees were in complete agreement – first and foremost they were looking for people who were able to gain the respect of their teaching staff. They related this to the ability of principals to be on top of curriculum and pedagogy.

The New Zealand teacher seminar report makes very clear statements about the role of the principal in stimulating quality teaching (New Zealand Ministry of Education, 1993, pp. 25, 47 and 69):

> The principal is seen to be a key factor in the development and attribution of quality to teaching in a school. Principals, if they serve as role models of excellent teaching, can have a powerful influence through providing an exemplar of good practice and by creating a climate and expectation that all teaching performances should be meritorious. The group valued visionary leadership, a participative democracy, vitality, commitment, and drive in principals, but they also valued a caring approach and evidence of the "human" side of the principal. The principal was one who would tolerate experimentation, was supportive, was encouraging, who gave honest but positive feedback, who had an open door policy and who had clear, open lines of communication.
>
> For Principals do make a difference. They are critical in establishing school climate and in creating an environment conducive to quality teaching. Principals leading quality schools develop a vision and objectives for reaching the goals set. Such a function is not an expression of arrogance that the principal knows best and everyone must follow blindly the lead given. The vision must be shared both with the community of parents and with the staff to gain acceptance, support and ownership. It is a means whereby the energies of all can be harnessed and focused. The calibre of the principal is critical and is the principal's ability to construct a vision and to take the staff and the community along with the goals derived from that view of the educational future.

The Finnish case illustrates how the commitment to pupil progress and innovation permeates the administration and leadership of a school (Hämäläinen and Jokela, p. 18):

> It is a characteristic of the Jyväskylä University Training School that behind the success of its pupils there are many factors common to the whole school. In listing the factors which seem to explain the pupils' high school achievement, one common feature is the support the school offers the individual teacher. This comes from both the principal and from other staff. Care for the child's overall development is evident at the level of the individual teacher. It is difficult to form a general impression regarding teachers' interest in pupils' overall development by studying one single teacher.

The creation of opportunities for leadership is an important aspect of a school's provision for quality teachers. This illustration taken from a small rural school in England (Baker et al., p. 84) indicates the value of teachers being allocated a variety of leadership and administrative tasks:

> The work of a teacher in a small school is highly broad-based by nature. The teacher is required to take responsibility for such questions concerning school administration as the budget, planning of activity and contacts with school administrators, the school board and other teachers. The teacher should be familiar with matters related to building schools and pupil welfare. He must also be capable of functioning as the principal of a school. In addition to daily timetables, a teacher's work includes such matters as morning assemblies, supervision during breaks and school meals, and collaboration between the school and homes.

There are also a number of examples in the case studies of teachers who have assumed leadership roles as a consequence of their commitment to a vision of an individual child's development. The US case provides a number of illustrations of teachers outside the "hierarchy" who modified system policies in order to support individual students. Their ability to do this, however, was partially the result of flexibility and commitment to risk-taking that had been built into the school's norms. It seems that schools with high-quality teachers needs to provide a wide variety of contexts where informal and formal leadership can flourish. The final example from the Austrian case (Altrichter *et al.*, pp. 31-33) provides an excellent summary of this whole issue of leadership for school improvement:

> We have tried to discover what the characteristic strategies among the whole amount of staff interaction were. These are the *head's action strategies:*
> – formulating demands and stimulating initiative;
> – positive expectations and confidence in the staff's competence;
> – understanding and emotional backing;
> – initiating collaboration and exchange of ideas and materials;
> – concrete support;
> – little emphasis on administrative control;
> – "mistakes" are tolerated.

However, a head cannot make a good school on his or her own (although it is said that a head can make a school bad on his or her own). Thus, we must explore in what kind of *collegial* context the head's activities could evolve:
– some strong personalities among the staff;
– a "core group" supports the head's efforts;
– institutions for exchange and co-operation valued by staff;
– understanding, mutual stimulation, and emotional backing among staff.

Staff development

Although staff development is a key policy initiative for developing and sustaining teacher quality, and as such is dealt with in Chapter 5, it is also a fundamental feature of the "context of quality schooling". It is unlikely that schools without an infrastructure for staff development will be able to enhance the quality of their teachers. Many schools in the case studies developed "infrastructures" to support the professional development of staff. There are links here with specific policies for teacher quality such as teacher appraisal, as well as connections to other aspects of management arrangements such as planning and resource allocation.

For example, the New Zealand case study found (Ramsay, p. 71):
> *i)* Four of the five schools had well-developed systems of teacher appraisal and staff development. Contracts had been entered into between the principal and staff in order to fulfil the requirements of the system. In the fifth school, while

an appraisal scheme was not operating school wide, within the syndicate of the target teacher much work had been done in this respect.

ii) The teachers in the study agreed that the appraisal systems had led to more detailed reflection on their approaches and their curriculum knowledge, which, in turn had in their view, led to improved teaching practice.

iii) There was evidence that the schemes were operating well and that the teachers had been supported by personal and professional opportunities and by staff wide programmes which had improved both their pedagogy and their curriculum development.

Effective infrastructures contain a wide variety of activities that are able to respond to most teachers' developmental needs. This extract from the Japanese case study is illustrative (Maki, 1993, pp. 7–8):

The style of training for beginning teachers involves the following: lecture, workshop, seminar, practical exercise, study on teaching. [The] Voluntary-based Young Teacher Study Group (...) holds 20 [sessions] of training in which examination of teaching plans and demonstration of classroom teaching of the Group are conducted. In the process beginning teachers join the program. How to upgrade the teaching skills and to mitigate the anxiety which beginning teachers have because of less than six years of teaching experience, are main topics in the Group discussion. Such effort is very helpful for self-enlightenment toward the second year and onward of their career development.

The following description from the English case study gives a good illustration of the choice of staff development provision currently open to schools (Baker *et al.*, pp. 16-18):

The schools defined professional development activities in a number of ways: from award-bearing courses to team-teaching. One primary school listed a range of possibilities in its staff development policy statement, including both the traditional and the more unusual, for example, weekend residential conferences involving all teachers in the school.

With devolved budgets, schools were considering, perhaps more carefully than hitherto, not only their training needs but also the kinds of provision they wished to use and at what cost. All were committed to using a range of providers, locations and modes, though the exploration of options was rarely systematic. The LEA [local education authority], however, remained the dominant providers.

Where schools had been disappointed with the quality of provision it was often because there was a mismatch between their expectations and those of the providers. One remedy was perceived to be more bespoke courses or events; another, more time to shop around for suitable provision and providers. But there was also a general feeling that an increased use should be made of the expertise of a school's own staff, sometimes ignoring the parochialism this might engender.

Within the LEA certain teachers and senior managers were becoming known as experts in particular fields. The benefits derived from this local expertise had, however, to be set against the effects on the school of the frequent absence of particular teachers or managers.

A continuing difficulty with contemporary schemes for staff development is the stress they place on the organisation of a school. The following extract from the English case (p. 20) illustrates the point well. It is, however, worth adding that some schools, in the belief that staff development is the key to teacher quality, have managed to be very creative in "finding time" for staff development:

> The release of staff to undertake professional development during teaching time, either in or outside the school, was dependent on the often limited availability of supply teachers and/or flexible staffing arrangements; for example, in one primary school, the deputy head teacher was given the time and scope to work alongside other teachers, to release them for training and also to free co-ordinators to support other staff. In another school a part-time teacher's contract included covering for two groups of staff so they could be freed from teaching duties. Head teachers sometimes replaced teachers who were undertaking training. Such arrangements ensured that pupils received consistent teaching from teachers who were familiar with individual pupils and the context in which they were learning. However, it was not always clear that the cost effectiveness of these staffing arrangements had been considered.

There is an unfortunate tendency in the context of centralised reform for policy makers to regard "staff development" or "in-service" as a "treatment" for teachers responsible for implementing new ideas. Concern is expressed by a number of case-study writers that an overly bureaucratic or systems approach to in-service teacher education (INSET) is counterproductive. Consider this discussion of the use of study days in the Swedish case (Lander, p. 146):

> Before leaving the study-day issue it may be concluded that much of their bad reputation was due to school leaders and municipal planners relying on a pedagogy favouring lecturing, and with no idea of the follow-up. Unfortunately the lecturers themselves too often accepted playing the role given to them. The market situation for a time was such that easy INSET solutions could easily be sold. It was the time when state resources for INSET were massively transmitted to municipal control. The buyers at the market got too much money in relation to their restricted conceptions about what could be done with the money. At the same time, alternative thinking was often blocked by teacher groups competing for just their own categories' aims.

The point is further made in the Swedish case (p. 142), that with more complex innovations, schools:

- need to engage in longer developmental tasks, and make priorities of resources in accordance to that;
- need to trust that teachers spontaneously take care of educational ideas, try them out and share them with colleagues in such a way that the whole staff, or parts of it, learn to use them.

As a matter of fact, these are the solutions used at the schools in our samples. We can, however, see some important differences among schools and departments. The very idea of adopting a new organisational form for instruction, auch as non-grading, block-teaching or increased internal choice, puts heavy demands on teachers to learn and to invent. The joint responsibility also tends to increase mutual commitment and mutual assistance in learning. The need to adapt to the new organisation and its founding ideas opens up for new ideas among most teachers. Such investments in organisation also ought to increase the likelihood that "hard money" will be spent when the initial "soft moneys" on training was spent.

Staff development is, therefore, a complex and necessary activity for ensuring high levels of teacher quality in schools. At its most successful, staff development assumes forms that promote student progress. They are also supportive of the forms of teacher collaboration so characteristic of teacher quality that were described in detail earlier.

Relationships with the community and district

Many of the successful schools described in the case studies have established powerful links with, and are responsive to, their communities from which they generate some of their core values. Relationships with external agencies also appear important for sustaining teacher quality.

There is, however, a paradox here. The tide of national reforms currently sweeping most OECD countries with their emphasis on decentralisation and school autonomy put increased control for education into the hands of local people. At the same time, however, these policies are eroding the local level of support. The reduced role of the local education authority in England and Wales is a paradigmatic example of this phenomenon. At one and the same time, schools are being entreated to become more responsive to their communities but the support to enable them to do this is being withdrawn. This is not, however, the case in every country or case study. Nor is it a major focus of this study. Despite this it is evident that a positive "loose-figure" relationship between school and district is a characteristic of effective schools. The US case that focuses on the role of Fairfax County School District provides, as was seen earlier, a striking presentation of a strong and supportive relationship at the school-district level.

The other aspect of this issue is the school's relationship with its community. It would appear a truism from the case studies that strong community links are a feature of schools with high levels of teacher quality. The following two examples from the Finnish (Kimonen and Nevalainen, 1993, p. 91) and New Zealand (Ramsay, pp. 66-67) case studies are sufficient to illustrate the point:

Finland – The case-study school has become an important meeting place for the village community. The facilities and the equipment of the school are used efficiently also in the evenings and during weekends. The many-sided use of the school building for the villagers' leisure-time activities has taken place without problems, according to the teachers. Because the school has mainly been repaired with the help of voluntary work, responsibility is taken for its maintenance as well. The many activities of the parents and other inhabitants in the village presuppose that the teacher has an ability to co-operate, is adaptable and open.

"Yes, the school keeps this kind of a small village together. If it disappeared a lot would also change. Then we should have some other place where to have these village meetings and other things. Without the school, many other things would die. I think also these hobbies that have been arranged in the school" (pupil's mother).

"I haven't heard anyone complaining. Even the cleaning lady can arrange cleaning at a proper time, when she knows the program. There is still room for some stimulating activities for the old after school. When a taxi takes the pupils home, the old could come there to have one of their meetings. The village people have fixed up the school building so that it can be used" (teacher, female).

New Zealand – The schools involved in this study, as already noted, had very strong community involvement. At Countryside, for example, it was noted that the school had long been the focus of the community. Children currently attending were often fourth generation students at the school. In his interview, the principal told me that there was very little problem in obtaining help from parents in fund-raising ventures, in working bees or other activities which supported the school. While not recording the same level of community support, all of the other schools had very heavy parental involvement in a variety of ways. Most typically these were to help the school raise funds but there was also involvement of parents in curriculum decision making at each of the schools. In my field notes I noted a very high level of adult involvement in both classroom and school matters. The schools were never short of adult help in either scholastic or other ventures.

The Boards of Trustees [BOTs] at each of the schools also made sure that there regular visitors to the schools. At Countryside the Chairperson visited at least once a week, which appeared to be about the average for most of the schools. At Queenwood the Chairperson shared morning tea with the staff regularly – his emphasis on the informal contact was reflected by other Chairpersons. The interview data showed clearly that the principals and staff enjoyed a high level of support from their respective BOTs.

Culture of the school

The culture of the school is not distinct from any of the other aspects of the "context of schooling". It is, however, the least tangible. The culture of the school is at one and the same time the most powerful influence on teacher quality, yet the most difficult to affect. A positive school culture is what evolves when all the aspects of the context of schooling described in this chapter are in place. One key element identified in the case studies is encouragement of risk-taking and collaborative experimentation. A supportive culture for teacher quality thrives on a strong vision of student progress, powerful conceptions of teaching, and extensive teacher collaboration supported by an imaginative and flexible infrastructure at the school level.

The following extracts from the English case study (Baker *et al.*, p. 25) describes the important yet nebulous quality of a school's culture:

These (bureaucratic) conditions were not, however, determinants of effective professional development. At the end of the day it was teachers' awareness of need and their perception of the quality and relevance of training which appeared to count most.

Staff claimed that many outcomes could not be measured but that these were, nonetheless, vital to their professional development; for example, an ability to work more effectively with other teachers – to feel and act as part of a team; to analyse with more certainty aspects of classroom practice and to plan accordingly with greater precision. Many just felt more enthusiastic about the job.

The success of government policy depends to a considerable extent on schools' ability to manage change. One school had invested a major part of its training budget on preparing the whole staff to change direction, philosophically and practically. The new ethos is characterised by staff who are more flexible, productively self-critical and responsive to further national initiatives.

The Austrian case study (Altrichter *et al.*, p. 31) well captures the concept of culture that "glues together" the other aspects of the context of school. This phenomenon is frequently found in those case-study schools committed to high teacher quality:

In school V (a primary school) there are certainly some "competent and strong teacher personalities" who have contributed to the development of the school's specific qualities. On the other hand, a mother's judgement seems plausible that the characteristic of the school is not primarily "achievements of single teachers" but also a "spirit of the school" which is represented for parents by most staff.

It does not make a difference to which teacher one is talking in this school. It's the spirit of the school (...). The child as a human being is really in the centre of their thinking. One is feeling that also with small matters: when you hear them talking about children – there is simply a very positive general tones.

What are the specific features of this "spirit of the school"? Our interviewees, parents, teachers, head and inspector, identified the following strengths of the school: Most prominently, there is the *special early reading and writing teaching approach* which starts with whole words which are provided and "owned" by the children. This teaching strategy fits well and is interwoven with the general aim of the school to provide a *child-centred education which is appropriate to the individual development and which also offers psychological care*. Thirdly, it is typical for the school that teachers show a high degree of *commitment, activity and engagement*. Not all staff have exactly the same style of teaching, some are doing much project work and open classroom work while others work more conventionally; however, they are similar in that they highly regard initiative and are committed to fostering the children's development. Fourthly, the school is keen on developing *intensive parent-teacher-relationships*, which has led to the design of a successful type of parents' evening in which educational topics chosen by the parents are discussed in a "didactic setting" devised and managed by the teacher. Fifthly, the school is renowned for *whole-school activities and an high profile in the public*. Sixthly, there are some special musical activities; and seventhly, there is a special *staff climate* which is both characterised by *collegiality* and a *purposeful management*.

It is these features of the school context that underpin this final graphic example from the US case study (White and Roesch, pp. 137-38) of a school culture where teacher quality thrives and flourishes:

> I am greeted at the door by the Queen of Hearts and as I watch, the early bus begins to discharge pirates, princesses and pigs. It's Story Character Day at Meadowlark Elementary and the faculty, students and parents are dressed as their favourite storybook character.
>
> I follow the Queen of Hearts (aka the reading specialist) into the media centre where the morning broadcast is being produced live on closed circuit T.V. A fourth, third and second grade student dressed in imaginative costumes are asked to enter the "studio" and the Queen of Hearts, with no sense of urgency, tension or hysteria efficiently prepares them to go on the morning T.V. program. She says, "Let's rehearse. Can you all say together "Happy Story Character Day"? After the students chorus this, she then instructs them to tell their name and then say, "Can you guess who I am?" Seconds later the show goes on the air and the guest characters perform with admirable aplomb. The sixth grade anchors smoothly read the morning announcements and give a weather report complete with pointer and Virginia map. When I ask about the performance later on, I am told that it is the philosophy of the school to have students gain experience communicating with different technology, (thereby enhancing competence and their self-esteem) rather than having adults do all the talking.
>
> While I am at the school I attend almost daily teacher meetings and workshops in which teaching strategies and materials are shared. Sunny, warm, inviting, the school is such a pleasant place for all who enter – students, teachers, visitors and parents are acknowledged with smiles, encouraged and courteously listened to... I also find out that a first grade teacher is conducting a county in-service course on cooperative learning at the school. I note how readily teachers at this school change roles. On one day they may be a learner at a presentation on math tool boxes and the next day they may be teachers of teachers.
>
> This faculty takes risks! They aggressively pursued school restructuring after much research and planning. This faculty reads professional literature and connects theory to practice. When I expressed (true) ignorance of school restructuring, I was instantly given five recent research articles from national journals. Members of the faculty have since given local, state and national presentations on this topic.
>
> On Tuesday I attend a very early morning steering committee meeting. As teachers are working their way through the agenda and making decisions about student awards, an exciting "philosophical disagreement" breaks out. Teachers are polite, courteous, animated but not afraid to speak their own minds as they consider whether competition, which some advocate as "preparing students to live in the real world" can co-exist with their goals of developing a cooperative school community. I am impressed: in-depth reflection on core beliefs and how they should be enacted in the school's daily activities – and all before 7.30 in the morning!

Summary and conclusions

There are four general but powerful conclusions to be drawn from this review of the country case studies on the context of schooling.

The first is how consistent the case studies are in unfolding their stories of what are the key internal conditions and more general contexts required for schools that have high-quality teachers. The second is how consistent the conclusions that can be drawn from the case studies are with the research base, briefly reviewed in preceding chapters, on school effectiveness, improvement, and policy implementation. The third is how the individual factors identified as constituting the context of schooling do not exist in isolation. Rather, they operate as gestalt or braid that takes on unique forms in different schools. Teacher quality, it appears, is enhanced as a result of a holistic approach to school improvement.

Fourth, "teacher quality" in the way it has been defined in this project and described in these case studies is a consequence of deliberate action and commitment by individual teachers at the classroom and school level rather than as a result of the demand for enhanced teacher quality through external or top-down policy initiatives. It appears on the basis of these case studies that the success of policy implementation is a function of the "goodness of fit" between the fundamental beliefs of teachers and the values of the school and the policy being implemented.

There are five key characteristics of the contexts of those schools described in these case studies that exhibit unusually *high levels of teacher quality:*

- *a clear vision or moral purpose* that has the progress of all students, irrespective of their learning histories, at its core: teachers believe they can and will make a difference to the life chances of all their pupils;
- a commitment to *collaborative teacher development* not necessarily as an end in itself but as the most direct means to ensuring the success of all students;
- an *investment in high-quality teachers* on the part of the school: this applies to recruitment and staff development policies, as well as the resourcing of collaborative activities, the encouragement of "risk-taking" and "leadership" at all levels of the school;
- a modification of the schools' *management arrangements* or internal organisational conditions to create an infrastructure within the school supportive of high-quality teaching and learning: this takes many different forms in different countries, but usually involves a commitment to school-based development planning, the use of teams and informal networks, increased communication and broader involvement in decision-making;
- a *symbiotic relationship between the school, its district authority and community*: this involves pressure and support at all levels within a context of shared educational values.

These five key characteristics, although comprising an ideal type of school context, reflect the day-to-day reality of many schools described in the country case studies. However, these schools represent a selected sample of schools with higher than average levels of both quality teachers and quality teaching. The key question, as the Australian case-study writer noted in the concluding sentence of his report, is how these conditions can be translated into an enduring and widely supported policy framework. We take up this question in the next chapter.

Chapter 7

Sources of Teacher Quality

In this chapter we consider alternative approaches to improving teacher quality. Chapter 4 explained how the conception of teacher quality agreed upon at the beginning of the project did not entirely fit the evidence subsequently produced by the country studies, because it was too static. The new conception emerging from the case studies and teacher seminars is more dynamic: the nature of good teaching changes in response to new kinds of students, new theories and evidence about human learning, new technologies, and new roles for teachers and schools. This makes policy formulation more difficult because teacher quality is a moving target.

The description in Chapter 5 of policies that have been promulgated to improve the quality of teachers and teaching indicates that policy makers have taken on board some of the conclusions from research on policy implementation. For example, in-service training for teachers now is often provided in support of new policies. However, the case studies indicate that there is still a long way to go. Policy implementation is strongly mediated, and occasionally stymied, by the local school context.

The dilemma, as discussed in Chapter 6, is that strong schools – the ones that support high-quality teaching – have their own priorities. Their strength and effectiveness stems in part from the very fact that they have a clear, shared vision of their own purpose and method. Shared values are tempered and tested daily in the interactions among students, school staff, and the outside community. They are built into the organisation of teaching and learning, and into management arrangements that determine how teachers work with their colleagues. They are part of a school culture. These shared values, commitments, and ways of working cannot be easily changed by a new policy or programme issued by central authorities. However, if the policy or programme is consistent with the school's own priorities, the school may make good and effective use of it.

Three sources of quality

Initiatives to improve teacher quality thus spring from individual teachers, individual schools, and external policies enacted by local, regional, or national education authorities. (We do not discuss here the relations among these different levels of authority external to the school.) The problem is how to arrange for these initiatives to complement and reinforce one another, not conflict and compete. As a start, it is useful to consider each of these sources in isolation, and the kinds of policies apt to be most congenial to it. We thus sketch three brief scenarios.

Source 1: The individual teacher. Teacher quality springs from individual teachers' motivations and capacities. Gifted teachers create excellence almost regardless of what is going on around them. Glimpses of such teachers appear in the country studies from New Zealand (Ramsay, 1993), Italy (Macconi, 1993), the United States (White and Roesch, 1993), and Sweden (Lander, 1993).

In this scenario teacher quality resides in individual teachers. Their teaching is characterised by grace and fluidity as they orchestrate the classroom in a seemingly effortless way. They are so confident in what they are doing that they are able to pace the lesson, utilise a variety of teaching strategies and control the tempo of learning to meet the needs of individuals and groups. The classroom is a happy place, students are challenged but secure, excited and motivated by the learning opportunities that surround them. The classroom itself has a vibrancy to it, with the tables and chairs rearranged to suit different teaching situations and the displays that celebrate the work of students changing as the themes of the lessons evolve.

Despite the natural feel to the classroom, these teachers work hard within and outside the lesson. Their confidence is underpinned by thorough preparation and deep understanding. Although these teachers collaborate with other colleagues, they also choose to work alone. Their collaboration is usually for a specific purpose as they seek out other colleagues from whom they can learn. Similarly, they take in-service courses and engage in professional development, not just for their own sake but because the course or opportunity contributes directly to their own learning. If these opportunities are not readily available, or if what is on offer is insufficient, they will seek out alternatives.

To the extent that teacher quality rests on individual initiative and skill, the policy implications include:

- rigorous selection procedures which admit only high-quality entrants to the profession;
- pre-service teacher education that is short, challenging, and as much as possible practice-based;
- a relatively high level of financial remuneration;
- career progression that rewards excellence in teaching and keeps good teachers in the classroom;
- an array of challenging professional development opportunities that allow individual choice;
- a school organisation that fosters individual autonomy;
- a policy environment that is enabling rather than constraining.

Source 2: The individual school. Teacher quality springs from schools organised with infrastructures that support good teaching and collaboration among teachers. Within the school, conditions have been created specifically to support the teaching and learning process; and more generally at an organisational level to establish frameworks, create roles, allocate responsibilities, and generate ways of working that reflect the shared educational values of the school. Depictions of these school-level dynamics appear in the country reports from Australia (McRae, 1993), Austria (Altrichter *et al.*, 1993), England (Baker *et al.*, 1993), Finland (Hämäläinen and Jokela, 1993), and the United States (White and Roesch, 1993).

In this scenario the source of teacher quality appears to be the school. As one enters the building a sense of purpose abounds. Irrespective of its age the school appears attractive and, although movement is orderly, there is a sense of energy to the place. Evidence of success abounds and a feel for the school's values can be gleaned from the displays in hallways and other shared spaces. Talk to the students and most remark that it is a friendly place, that they enjoy coming to school and that they feel "pushed" in their lessons. Talk to the teachers and they speak well of the students, their colleagues and the school teachers. They are clear about their educational purposes and one soon gets the impression that collaboration is the customary practice.

Talk to the school leaders and the conversation initially centres around students. One soon realises that the school's values, which the teachers referred to, are also represented in its organisational structures. Attempts are being made to reduce the hierarchy so common in many schools; teams and a developmental approach to appraisal are evident. Meetings on bureaucratic matters are kept to a minimum, with more time being given to discussion of curriculum and teaching. There are wide-ranging opportunities given to staff development from within and outside the school. The school uses its planning procedures and structures for developmental work, and is keen to adapt initiatives from the outside for their own purposes.

Talk to inspectors and they report high quality and consistent teaching, an orderly environment and good management systems. Talk to parents and they are pleased their child is a student, they report high expectations, as well as a caring attitude on the part of staff.

To the extent that teacher quality rests on school-level factors, the policy implications are:
- pre-service education of new teachers that is to a large extent school-based;
- decentralisation of management and budget to the school level;
- a reduction of control over school governance by the local (district) level;
- specificity in policy directives yet with high levels of support and the opportunity to adapt and experiment;
- a responsive system of external support surrounding the school that includes both inspection and advice;
- creation of networks of like-minded schools to exchange information and support;
- opportunities for schools to have a say in curriculum decision-making and to adapt mandated curricula to the local situation;
- the encouragement of self evaluation and planning at the school level;
- flexibility in provision of INSET (in-service teacher education) and staff development.

Source 3: *The external policy environment.* Teacher quality is the result of coherent and well-tested policies relating pre-service and in-service teacher education, curriculum, student assessment and teacher appraisal. Educational excellence depends on faithful implementation of these policies, not on independent initiatives of individual teachers or schools. Examples of strong central policy initiatives are given in the case studies from Italy (Macconi, 1993), Japan (Maki, 1993), England (Baker *et al.*, 1993), and the United States (White and Roesch, 1993).

In this scenario the central authority publicly acknowledges its responsibility for teacher quality. It introduces a wide-ranging series of curriculum reforms reflecting core societal values and key skills. At the same time systems for inspection of schools are more rigorously applied. Emphasis is increasingly placed on assessment, and grade-level criteria are widely disseminated.

At the school level, administrators are increasingly held accountable for meeting centrally defined standards. Teacher evaluation systems reflect central rather than individual values. Teacher education programmes nationally are widely scrutinised, and schemes for accreditation established. More public accountability for teacher education is also introduced. The public are in general pleased that firm action is being taken.

To the extent that teacher quality rests on central authorities, the policy implications are:
- a clear public mandate for executive action;
- consultative procedures in formation of policy;
- a broad and coherent range of complementary policy options;
- a central inspectorate to monitor the progress of individual schools;
- a central system of teacher evaluation;
- teacher education that complements the direction of the reforms;
- central support to assist in implementation;
- an information system and vocabulary to generate public debate on education.

Reconciling teacher, school, and central policy

It should be obvious that no one of these cases is realistic by itself. They are intended to starkly illustrate the range of policy options implicit in the case studies and teacher seminar reports, and to point out the conflicts that exist. For example, individual teachers must necessarily have less autonomy if they are required to adhere to central policies regarding curriculum and instructional methods, or if they must participate with colleagues in their school in seeking consensus about values and practices. Because of their singularity, these three scenarios thus underscore the complexity and problematic nature of policy choice in this area. To the extent that each scenario is unrealistic and unacceptable, the policy options become more complex. Each of these scenarios has its attractions and disadvantages.

The first scenario that focuses on the individual teacher is on the one hand the most appealing because of the powerful imagery of teaching and teachers that it conveys. On the other hand, it is also problematic. Teachers find it difficult to sustain their energy and enthusiasm over time without a support structure around them. Also, teachers who work in isolation may miss opportunities to learn from colleagues and therefore never fulfil their own potential as teachers. Inept or unmotivated teachers cannot be left to their own devices. Relying on individual teachers seems most viable in settings where teachers are granted reasonably high levels of societal respect and institutional authority.

The second scenario that reflects the school-level emphasis will be attractive to a number of countries because it reflects the current policy trend towards decentralisation and "site-based management". The school-level model has the advantage of fostering consistency among teachers within each school, regarding both teaching methods and behavioural expectations for students. However, collaborative arrangements are vulnerable to turnover of personnel: if a key person leaves, a team may collapse. Intense collaboration and constant communication also take a substantial amount of time, which may detract from time in the classroom. Furthermore, the creation of school structures and cultures that epitomise this ideal type is difficult, as the school improvement literature illustrates.

The third scenario is one that some OECD countries have been embracing, while others move away from it. Some countries with a tradition of central control have been devolving responsibility to local schools in an attempt to stimulate innovation adapted to local circumstances. At the same time, certain countries that lack a tradition of central control are trying to raise standards of student performance through policies of coherent systemic change orchestrated from the centre. The advantage of coherent, centralised policy control is that it can create consistency from one school to another. The disadvantage is that policies, once in place, can be difficult to change. When curriculum, assessment, pre-service and in-service teacher education are all connected, there is a great deal of inertia. Reliance on central policy may therefore increase the difficulty of capturing the dynamic nature of teacher quality, which is one of the main ideas emerging from the country studies. For example, as constructivist theories of learning have come to dominate educational psychology, certain centralised systems have been slow to respond, in spite of some teachers' desire to adopt more student-centred forms of pedagogy.

We close, therefore, with a conundrum. Relying on central policy to sustain and improve teacher quality implies greater consistency of practice but a slower rate of change. In contrast, relying on individual teachers and schools allows continuous change and experimentation, but also permits some schools and teachers to lag far behind. The big challenge is to improve the terms of this trade-off by channelling together the different sources of teacher quality.

Bibliography

ALMIUS, T., LANDER, R. and ODHAGEN, T. (1993), "Instruction and relations – reflections over two seminars with teachers from comprehensive schools in Sweden", Department of Education and Educational Research, University of Linköping.

ALTRICHTER, H., AMMANN, U., RADNITZY, E. and SPECHT, W. (1993), "Case studies on teacher quality", Department of Business Education and Personnel Management, University of Innsbruck, Austria.

ALTET, M. (1993), "La qualité des enseignants, séminaires d'enseignants. Rapport final de l'étude française demandée par la Direction de l'Évaluation et de la Prospective", Centre de recherches en éducation, Université de Nantes (DEP9, CREN).

ASKLING, B. and JEDESKOG, G. (1993), "The teacher education review: some notes on the Teacher Education Programme in Sweden", Department of Education and Psychology, University of Linköping.

BAASLAND, B. (1993), "Teacher quality. The national case study", Royal Ministry of Education, Research and Church Affairs, Oslo, Norway.

BAKER, C.A., MUSCHAMP, P. and DRACUP, T. (1993), "Teacher quality: English case study", Office for Standards in Education and Department for Education, London.

BARBIER, J-M. and GALATANU, O. (1993), "La qualité des enseignants. L'examen des programmes de formation des enseignants", Conservatoire National des Arts et Métiers, Centre de Recherche sur la Formation, Paris.

BIGWOOD, W.F.L. (1993), "Teacher education programme review, Scotland", Moray House Institute of Education, Edinburgh.

BRADLEY, A. (1993), "Teacher education and standards", *Education Week*, November 24.

BUCHBERGER, F. (ed.) (1992), *ATEE-Guide to Institutions of Teacher Education in Europe (AGITE)*, Association for Teacher Education in Europe (ATEE), Brussels.

BUCHBERGER, F., NIEMI, H., KOHONEN, V., ROTHBUCHER, H., THONHAUSER, J. and VÄHÄPASSI, A. (1993), "Teacher education programme review. Austria", State College of Teacher Education in Salzburg, Institute of Educational Sciences/University of Salzburg.

BUCHBERGER, F., NIEMI, H., KOHONEN, V., ROTHBUCHER, H., THONHAUSER, J. and VÄHÄPASSI, A. (1993a), "Report of the teacher education programme review", University of Jyväskylä, Finland.

CARNEGIE FORUM ON EDUCATION AND THE ECONOMY (1986), *A Nation Prepared: Teachers for the 21st Century*, New York.

COMMONWEALTH TERTIARY EDUCATION COMMISSION (CTEC) (1986), *Improving Teacher Education*, Joint Review of Teacher Education and Commonwealth Schools Commission, Canberra.

CROSS, P.K. (1984), "The rising tide of reform reports", *Phi Delta Kappan*, 65.

DEPARTMENT FOR EDUCATION (1992), "Induction of newly qualified teachers", Administrative Memorandum 2/92, 11 August, London.

DEPARTMENT OF EMPLOYMENT, EDUCATION AND TRAINING (DEET) (1992), "Teacher education. A discussion paper", Canberra.

EKHOLM, M., FRANSSON, A. and LANDER, R. (1987), *Skolreform ock lokalt gensvar, Utvärdering av 35 grundskolor genom upprepade lägesbedömningar 1980-1985* (School Reform and Local Response, Evaluation of 35 Comprehensive Schools by Successive Assessments), Institutionen för Pedagogik, Göteborgs Universitet.

FULLAN, M. (1985), "Change processes and strategies at the local level", *The Elementary School Journal*, 3.

HÄMÄLÄINEN, S. and JOKELA, J. (eds.) (1993), "Teacher quality in Finland: policy and practice in five primary schools. Summary of case studies", *Research*, 54, Department of Teacher Education, University of Jyväskylä, Finland.

HARGREAVES, D.H. and HOPKINS, D. (1991), *The Empowered School*, Cassell, London.

HOLMES GROUP (1986), *Tomorrows' Teachers*, East Lansing, MI.

HOPKINS, D. (ed.) (1986), *Inservice Training and Educational Development*, Croom Helm, London.

HOPKINS, D. (1987), *Improving the Quality of Schooling*, Falmer Press, Lewes.

HOPKINS, D. (1990), "The International School Improvement Project (ISIP) and effective schooling: towards a synthesis", *School Organisation*, 10 (2 and 3).

ITALIAN MINISTRY OF EDUCATION (1992), "Teacher quality: Country statement: Italy", First Japan/OECD Seminar on Teacher Education and the Quality of Schooling, Saitama Prefecture, Tokyo, February.

KIMONEN, F. and NEVALAINEN, R. (1993), "The teacher of a small rural school implementing the local curriculum. A case study of the Sointula Lower Level Comprehensive School, Central Finland", in S. Hämäläinen and J. Jokela (eds.), *op. cit.*, pp. 75-100 (pre-publication draft).

LANDER, R. (1993), "Repertoires of teaching quality. A contribution to the OECD/CERI project Teacher Quality from case studies of six Swedish comprehensive schools", Department of Education and Educational Science, University of Göteborg.

LIEBERMAN, A. and MILLER, L. (eds.) (1978), *Staff Development: New Demands, New Realities, New Perspectives*, New York.

MACCONI, C. (1993), "Teacher quality project: Italian case study", Ministero Pubblica Istruzione, Direzione Generale Scambi Culturali, Rome.

MAKI, M. (1992), "Changing pattern of work organization and the quality of teaching, Japan", National Institute for Educational Research, Tokyo.

MAKI, M. (1992a), "Improving teacher quality in Japan", National Institute for Educational Research, Tokyo.

MAKI, M. (1993), "A case study on induction training for beginning teachers in Japan", National Institute for Educational Research, Tokyo.

McLAUGHLIN, M. (1990), "The Rand Change Agent Study revisited: macro perspectives, micro realities", *Educational Researcher*, 19 (9).

McRAE, D. (1993), "Reforming school work organisation: Australia", Department of Employment, Education and Training, Commonwealth Government of Australia, Canberra.

NATIONAL CENTER FOR EDUCATIONAL STATISTICS (1991), *Digest of Education Statistics 1991*, Government Printing Office, Washington.

NATIONAL BOARD FOR PROFESSIONAL TEACHING STANDARDS (NBPTS) (1991), *Toward High and Rigorous Standards for the Teaching Profession*, 3rd edition, Detroit and Washington.

NEW ZEALAND MINISTRY OF EDUCATION, (1993), "The New Zealand report on teacher quality seminars", Wellington.

NORWAY MINISTRY OF EDUCATION (1993), "Teacher quality: Case studies", Oslo.

OECD (1974), *The Teacher and Educational Change: A New Role*, OECD, Paris.

OECD (1979), *Teacher Policies in a New Context*, OECD, Paris.

OECD (1982), *In-Service Education and Training of Teachers: A Condition for Educational Change*, OECD, Paris.

OECD (1989), "Decentralisation and school improvement: new perspectives and conditions for change", CERI/CD(89)4, OECD, Paris.

OECD (1989a), *Schools and Quality: An International Report*, OECD, Paris.

OECD (1990), *The Teacher Today: Tasks, Conditions, Policies*, OECD, Paris.

OECD (1992), *High-Quality Education and Training for All*, OECD, Paris.

PURKEY, S.C. and SMITH, M. (1983), "Effective schools – a review", *The Elementary School Journal*, 4, pp. 427-452.

RAMSAY, P. (1993), "Teacher quality. A case study prepared for the Ministry of Education as part of the OECD study on teacher quality", University of Waikato, Hamilton, New Zealand.

RIBOLITS, E. (1993), "Final report on the teacher seminars conducted as part of the OECD study on teacher quality", Vocational Teacher Training Academy for Agriculture and Forestry, Vienna, Austria (in co-operation with Mrs. Edith Gaderer-Witerna).

ROSENHOLTZ, S. (1989), *Teachers Workplace: The Social Organisation of Schools*, Longman, New York.

SCHÖN, D.A. (1983), *The Reflective Practitioner*, Temple Smith, London.

SCOTTISH EDUCATION DEPARTMENT (1992), "Teacher quality, country contribution: United Kingdom (Scotland)", Edinburgh.

SLAVIN, R.E. (1993), "Cooperative learning in OECD countries: research, practice, and prevalence", Center for Research on Effective Schooling for Disadvantaged Students, Johns Hopkins University, Baltimore, MD.

TALBERT, J.E. and McLAUGHLIN, M.V. (1994), "Teacher professionalism in broad schools contexts", *American Journal of Education*, 102.

VAN VELZEN, W., MILES, M., EKHOLM, M., HAMEYER, U. and ROBIN, D. (1985), *Making School Improvement Work*, ACCO, Leuven, Belgium.

WAGNER, A. (forthcoming), "The Economics of Teacher Education", *International Encyclopaedia of Education*, 2nd edition.

WHITE, J.J. and ROESCH, M. (1993), "Listening to the voices of teachers: examining connections between student performance, quality of teaching and educational policies in seven Fairfax County (VA) elementary and middle public schools", University of Maryland, Baltimore County, Fairfax County Public Schools, United States.

MAIN SALES OUTLETS OF OECD PUBLICATIONS
PRINCIPAUX POINTS DE VENTE DES PUBLICATIONS DE L'OCDE

ARGENTINA – ARGENTINE
Carlos Hirsch S.R.L.
Galería Güemes, Florida 165, 4° Piso
1333 Buenos Aires   Tel. (1) 331.1787 y 331.2391
                    Telefax: (1) 331.1787

AUSTRALIA – AUSTRALIE
D.A. Information Services
648 Whitehorse Road, P.O.B 163
Mitcham, Victoria 3132   Tel. (03) 873.4411
                         Telefax: (03) 873.5679

AUSTRIA – AUTRICHE
Gerold & Co.
Graben 31
Wien I   Tel. (0222) 533.50.14

BELGIUM – BELGIQUE
Jean De Lannoy
Avenue du Roi 202
B-1060 Bruxelles   Tel. (02) 538.51.69/538.08.41
                   Telefax: (02) 538.08.41

CANADA
Renouf Publishing Company Ltd.
1294 Algoma Road
Ottawa, ON K1B 3W8   Tel. (613) 741.4333
                     Telefax: (613) 741.5439
Stores:
61 Sparks Street
Ottawa, ON K1P 5R1   Tel. (613) 238.8985
211 Yonge Street
Toronto, ON M5B 1M4   Tel. (416) 363.3171
                      Telefax: (416)363.59.63
Les Éditions La Liberté Inc.
3020 Chemin Sainte-Foy
Sainte-Foy, PQ G1X 3V6   Tel. (418) 658.3763
                         Telefax: (418) 658.3763

Federal Publications Inc.
165 University Avenue, Suite 701
Toronto, ON M5H 3B8   Tel. (416) 860.1611
                      Telefax: (416) 860.1608

Les Publications Fédérales
1185 Université
Montréal, QC H3B 3A7   Tel. (514) 954.1633
                       Telefax : (514) 954.1635

CHINA – CHINE
China National Publications Import
Export Corporation (CNPIEC)
16 Gongti E. Road, Chaoyang District
P.O. Box 88 or 50
Beijing 100704 PR   Tel. (01) 506.6688
                    Telefax: (01) 506.3101

DENMARK – DANEMARK
Munksgaard Book and Subscription Service
35, Nørre Søgade, P.O. Box 2148
DK-1016 København K   Tel. (33) 12.85.70
                      Telefax: (33) 12.93.87

FINLAND – FINLANDE
Akateeminen Kirjakauppa
Keskuskatu 1, P.O. Box 128
00100 Helsinki
Subscription Services/Agence d'abonnements :
P.O. Box 23
00371 Helsinki   Tel. (358 0) 12141
                 Telefax: (358 0) 121.4450

FRANCE
OECD/OCDE
Mail Orders/Commandes par correspondance:
2, rue André-Pascal
75775 Paris Cedex 16   Tel. (33-1) 45.24.82.00
                       Telefax: (33-1) 49.10.42.76
                       Telex: 640048 OCDE

OECD Bookshop/Librairie de l'OCDE :
33, rue Octave-Feuillet
75016 Paris   Tel. (33-1) 45.24.81.67
              (33-1) 45.24.81.81
Documentation Française
29, quai Voltaire
75007 Paris   Tel. 40.15.70.00
Gibert Jeune (Droit-Économie)
6, place Saint-Michel
75006 Paris   Tel. 43.25.91.19
Librairie du Commerce International
10, avenue d'Iéna
75016 Paris   Tel. 40.73.34.60
Librairie Dunod
Université Paris-Dauphine
Place du Maréchal de Lattre de Tassigny
75016 Paris   Tel. (1) 44.05.40.13
Librairie Lavoisier
11, rue Lavoisier
75008 Paris   Tel. 42.65.39.95
Librairie L.G.D.J. - Montchrestien
20, rue Soufflot
75005 Paris   Tel. 46.33.89.85
Librairie des Sciences Politiques
30, rue Saint-Guillaume
75007 Paris   Tel. 45.48.36.02
P.U.F.
49, boulevard Saint-Michel
75005 Paris   Tel. 43.25.83.40
Librairie de l'Université
12a, rue Nazareth
13100 Aix-en-Provence   Tel. (16) 42.26.18.08
Documentation Française
165, rue Garibaldi
69003 Lyon   Tel. (16) 78.63.32.23
Librairie Decitre
29, place Bellecour
69002 Lyon   Tel. (16) 72.40.54.54

GERMANY – ALLEMAGNE
OECD Publications and Information Centre
August-Bebel-Allee 6
D-53175 Bonn   Tel. (0228) 959.120
               Telefax: (0228) 959.12.17

GREECE – GRÈCE
Librairie Kauffmann
Mavrokordatou 9
106 78 Athens   Tel. (01) 32.55.321
                Telefax: (01) 36.33.967

HONG-KONG
Swindon Book Co. Ltd.
13–15 Lock Road
Kowloon, Hong Kong   Tel. 366.80.31
                     Telefax: 739.49.75

HUNGARY – HONGRIE
Euro Info Service
Margitsziget, Európa Ház
1138 Budapest   Tel. (1) 111.62.16
                Telefax : (1) 111.60.61

ICELAND – ISLANDE
Mál Mog Menning
Laugavegi 18, Pósthólf 392
121 Reykjavik   Tel. 162.35.23

INDIA – INDE
Oxford Book and Stationery Co.
Scindia House
New Delhi 110001   Tel.(11) 331.5896/5308
                   Telefax: (11) 332.5993
17 Park Street
Calcutta 700016   Tel. 240832

INDONESIA – INDONÉSIE
Pdii-Lipi
P.O. Box 269/JKSMG/88
Jakarta 12790   Tel. 583467
                Telex: 62 875

ISRAEL
Praedicta
5 Shatner Street
P.O. Box 34030
Jerusalem 91430   Tel. (2) 52.84.90/1/2
                  Telefax: (2) 52.84.93
R.O.Y.
P.O. Box 13056
Tel Aviv 61130   Tél. (3) 49.61.08
                 Telefax (3) 544.60.39

ITALY – ITALIE
Libreria Commissionaria Sansoni
Via Duca di Calabria 1/1
50125 Firenze   Tel. (055) 64.54.15
                Telefax: (055) 64.12.57
Via Bartolini 29
20155 Milano   Tel. (02) 36.50.83
Editrice e Libreria Herder
Piazza Montecitorio 120
00186 Roma   Tel. 679.46.28
             Telefax: 678.47.51
Libreria Hoepli
Via Hoepli 5
20121 Milano   Tel. (02) 86.54.46
               Telefax: (02) 805.28.86
Libreria Scientifica
Dott. Lucio de Biasio 'Aeiou'
Via Coronelli, 6
20146 Milano   Tel. (02) 48.95.45.52
               Telefax: (02) 48.95.45.48

JAPAN – JAPON
OECD Publications and Information Centre
Landic Akasaka Building
2-3-4 Akasaka, Minato-ku
Tokyo 107   Tel. (81.3) 3586.2016
            Telefax: (81.3) 3584.7929

KOREA – CORÉE
Kyobo Book Centre Co. Ltd.
P.O. Box 1658, Kwang Hwa Moon
Seoul   Tel. 730.78.91
        Telefax: 735.00.30

MALAYSIA – MALAISIE
Co-operative Bookshop Ltd.
University of Malaya
P.O. Box 1127, Jalan Pantai Baru
59700 Kuala Lumpur
Malaysia   Tel. 756.5000/756.5425
           Telefax: 757.3661

MEXICO – MEXIQUE
Revistas y Periodicos Internacionales S.A. de C.V.
Florencia 57 - 1004
Mexico, D.F. 06600   Tel. 207.81.00
                     Telefax : 208.39.79

NETHERLANDS – PAYS-BAS
SDU Uitgeverij Plantijnstraat
Externe Fondsen
Postbus 20014
2500 EA's-Gravenhage   Tel. (070) 37.89.880
Voor bestellingen: Telefax: (070) 34.75.778

NEW ZEALAND
NOUVELLE-ZÉLANDE
Legislation Services
P.O. Box 12418
Thorndon, Wellington   Tel. (04) 496.5652
                       Telefax: (04) 496.5698

NORWAY – NORVÈGE
Narvesen Info Center – NIC
Bertrand Narvesens vei 2
P.O. Box 6125 Etterstad
0602 Oslo 6 Tel. (022) 57.33.00
 Telefax: (022) 68.19.01

PAKISTAN
Mirza Book Agency
65 Shahrah Quaid-E-Azam
Lahore 54000 Tel. (42) 353.601
 Telefax: (42) 231.730

PHILIPPINE – PHILIPPINES
International Book Center
5th Floor, Filipinas Life Bldg.
Ayala Avenue
Metro Manila Tel. 81.96.76
 Telex 23312 RHP PH

PORTUGAL
Livraria Portugal
Rua do Carmo 70-74
Apart. 2681
1200 Lisboa Tel.: (01) 347.49.82/5
 Telefax: (01) 347.02.64

SINGAPORE – SINGAPOUR
Gower Asia Pacific Pte Ltd.
Golden Wheel Building
41, Kallang Pudding Road, No. 04-03
Singapore 1334 Tel. 741.5166
 Telefax: 742.9356

SPAIN – ESPAGNE
Mundi-Prensa Libros S.A.
Castelló 37, Apartado 1223
Madrid 28001 Tel. (91) 431.33.99
 Telefax: (91) 575.39.98

Libreria Internacional AEDOS
Consejo de Ciento 391
08009 – Barcelona Tel. (93) 488.30.09
 Telefax: (93) 487.76.59

Llibreria de la Generalitat
Palau Moja
Rambla dels Estudis, 118
08002 – Barcelona
 (Subscripcions) Tel. (93) 318.80.12
 (Publicacions) Tel. (93) 302.67.23
 Telefax: (93) 412.18.54

SRI LANKA
Centre for Policy Research
c/o Colombo Agencies Ltd.
No. 300-304, Galle Road
Colombo 3 Tel. (1) 574240, 573551-2
 Telefax: (1) 575394, 510711

SWEDEN – SUÈDE
Fritzes Information Center
Box 16356
Regeringsgatan 12
106 47 Stockholm Tel. (08) 690.90.90
 Telefax: (08) 20.50.21

Subscription Agency/Agence d'abonnements :
Wennergren-Williams Info AB
P.O. Box 1305
171 25 Solna Tel. (08) 705.97.50
 Téléfax : (08) 27.00.71

SWITZERLAND – SUISSE
Maditec S.A. (Books and Periodicals - Livres
et périodiques)
Chemin des Palettes 4
Case postale 266
1020 Renens Tel. (021) 635.08.65
 Telefax: (021) 635.07.80

Librairie Payot S.A.
4, place Pépinet
CP 3212
1002 Lausanne Tel. (021) 341.33.48
 Telefax: (021) 341.33.45

Librairie Unilivres
6, rue de Candolle
1205 Genève Tel. (022) 320.26.23
 Telefax: (022) 329.73.18

Subscription Agency/Agence d'abonnements :
Dynapresse Marketing S.A.
38 avenue Vibert
1227 Carouge Tel.: (022) 308.07.89
 Telefax : (022) 308.07.99

See also – Voir aussi :
OECD Publications and Information Centre
August-Bebel-Allee 6
D-53175 Bonn (Germany) Tel. (0228) 959.120
 Telefax: (0228) 959.12.17

TAIWAN – FORMOSE
Good Faith Worldwide Int'l. Co. Ltd.
9th Floor, No. 118, Sec. 2
Chung Hsiao E. Road
Taipei Tel. (02) 391.7396/391.7397
 Telefax: (02) 394.9176

THAILAND – THAÏLANDE
Suksit Siam Co. Ltd.
113, 115 Fuang Nakhon Rd.
Opp. Wat Rajbopith
Bangkok 10200 Tel. (662) 225.9531/2
 Telefax: (662) 222.5188

TURKEY – TURQUIE
Kültür Yayinlari Is-Türk Ltd. Sti.
Atatürk Bulvari No. 191/Kat 13
Kavaklidere/Ankara Tel. 428.11.40 Ext. 2458
Dolmabahce Cad. No. 29
Besiktas/Istanbul Tel. 260.71.88
 Telex: 43482B

UNITED KINGDOM – ROYAUME-UNI
HMSO
Gen. enquiries Tel. (071) 873 0011
Postal orders only:
P.O. Box 276, London SW8 5DT
Personal Callers HMSO Bookshop
49 High Holborn, London WC1V 6HB
 Telefax: (071) 873 8200
Branches at: Belfast, Birmingham, Bristol, Edinburgh, Manchester

UNITED STATES – ÉTATS-UNIS
OECD Publications and Information Centre
2001 L Street N.W., Suite 700
Washington, D.C. 20036-4910 Tel. (202) 785.6323
 Telefax: (202) 785.0350

VENEZUELA
Libreria del Este
Avda F. Miranda 52, Aptdo. 60337
Edificio Galipán
Caracas 106 Tel. 951.1705/951.2307/951.1297
 Telegram: Libreste Caracas

Subscription to OECD periodicals may also be placed through main subscription agencies.

Les abonnements aux publications périodiques de l'OCDE peuvent être souscrits auprès des principales agences d'abonnement.

Orders and inquiries from countries where Distributors have not yet been appointed should be sent to: OECD Publications Service, 2 rue André-Pascal, 75775 Paris Cedex 16, France.

Les commandes provenant de pays où l'OCDE n'a pas encore désigné de distributeur devraient être adressées à : OCDE, Service des Publications, 2, rue André-Pascal, 75775 Paris Cedex 16, France.

9-1994

OECD PUBLICATIONS, 2 rue André-Pascal, 75775 PARIS CEDEX 16
PRINTED IN FRANCE
(96 94 07 1) ISBN 92-64-14242-8- No. 47481 1994

Ministry of Education & Training
MET Library
13th Floor, Mowat Block, Queen's Park
Toronto   M7A 1L2.